Stories

the World

Stories From Around the World

Edited by
Keith Danby

Authentic
LIFESTYLE

Copyright © 2002 Keith Danby

First published in 2002 by Authentic Lifestyle

08 07 06 05 04 03 02   7 6 5 4 3 2 1

Authentic Lifestyle is an imprint of
Authentic Media
PO Box 300, Carlisle, Cumbria, CA3 0QS, UK
and PO Box 1047, Waynesboro, GA 30830-2047, USA
www.paternoster-publishing.com

British Library Cataloguing in Publication Data
A catalogue record for this book is available from the
British Library

ISBN 1-85078-459-0

Cover design by Diane Bainbridge
Printed in Great Britain by
Cox and Wyman, Reading, Berkshire, RG1 8EX

Contents

Foreword

I was interviewed for my current job in February 1986 by Peter Maiden of Operation Mobilisation in a Pizza Hut just outside Euston Station in London. I was armed with five reasons why I was not the person OM were looking for and I only agreed to go for the interview out of courtesy to Peter, whom I had known for few years.

Although I was confident that I had clearly communicated that I did not have a vision to see Christian literature widely distributed and I honesty did not have a world vision, I was not convinced that Peter had changed his mind.

For the next 18 months, a little like Jonah, I ran as fast as I could, in the opposite direction to where God wanted me. I too had a crisis experience, not in the belly of a fish, but equally as forceful and by a miracle of God's grace he changed my heart and eventually submitted to the call and joined Send the Light in September 1987.

Since that time I have been involved most days in seeking to distribute Christian Resources – books, Bibles, music, videos and software – as widely as possible. The other passion of my life is God's mission to reach a world

with the love of Christ. This work has involved
me visiting India over 25 times and working
closely with a number of Christian organisations and mission agencies.

The idea of this book came out of that desire
to do more to motivate people to support mission work. The seed was planted in my mind
almost five years ago at one of our Christian
Media conferences when I heard reports of
what God was doing in several countries
around the world. All too frequently comes the
plea, 'if we only had more resources we could
accomplish so much more'. I am embarrassed
that it has taken so long to actually become a
reality.

Many of the contributors are people who
have become friends in recent years and I have
personally been inspired, stimulated and challenged by their written or spoken word. I am
particularly grateful to Philip, Rob and Jill for
responding so promptly to the request to be
involved in the project and clearly by adding
their names and material to the book gives it
huge credibility.

All the proceeds that Send the Light gets
from publishing and selling this book around
the world will go Christian organisations
involved in mission in the UK and overseas.
The print and production costs have even been
sponsored to maximise the contributions. I
hope the stories will stir and inspire you and

that the proceeds will help a little to fund some aspects of Christian mission.

Keith Danby, President /CEO
Send the Light, Carlisle, England

TEARFUND

Tearfund began its work in the 1960s. It is an evangelical Christian relief and development organisation working through local partners to bring help and hope to communities in need around the world. The Bible and historic evangelical understanding of its central truths remain its foundations. Tearfund is a founder member of the Jubilee 2000 Coalition and a member of the Disasters Emergency Committee of leading relief and development agencies.

Being the Hands and Face of Jesus

by Tim Hamilton and Doug Balfour with Sarah Chapman

When Josephine's husband came home he probably delivered her death sentence. She was glad to have him back, though she knew there was another woman. Sometimes he wouldn't be home for two or three nights.

'But he would at least buy me bread for the children,' says Josephine.

He died last year. Now she is sick and barely able to sit up for her visitors, the women from the local churches in Zambia, where she lives. In the quiet gloom of Josephine's one-room house the women perch on low stools and ask how she is.

'I'm depressed . . . My chest is bad. Sometimes I get sores in my mouth.'

Have her children eaten?

'Some small porridge this morning.'

Her arms are painfully thin; her face hollowed out by illness. She has been like this for four months. But she doesn't know what's wrong. Maybe TB, or asthma. Josephine hasn't been to the doctor. How could she? She has no money to feed her children.

The likelihood is that Josephine's husband gave her HIV, the virus that inevitably leads to Aids and death. No one talks about Aids here in Livingstone, a tourist town in the shadow of Victoria Falls. When you ask why someone died, they will say malaria, diarrhoea or tuberculosis. Yet almost every local language in Zambia has its own name for the illness that leaves you thin. Aids may be reaching its peak in Africa, but only because HIV has now infected so many people.

The world has never faced anything like this pandemic, and the worst is yet to come. In Zambia one in five people carry the virus. In other parts of Africa one in three are infected. Without testing or education, many of these will pass on HIV during the critical gap between infection and falling sick. A harvest of death across the continent is ripe. What has been sown in lack of resources and education will be reaped by a generation of children without parents.

Prevention is the only cure, but governments, churches and communities shy away from talking openly about sexual behaviour – the root cause of how quickly this virus spreads. Women are particularly vulnerable to infection, which is passed on mainly through heterosexual intercourse, and from mother to baby. Alleviating poverty and giving access to education and healthcare do make a difference – slowing the spread of HIV/Aids – particularly when women and mothers are involved. Uganda, the first African nation to acknowledge the problem openly, is also the first to see rates of infection come down.

Most African governments are now taking Aids seriously. But for many it's too late. And the problem of how to support the orphans left behind weighs heavily on communities that are already desperately poor.

Leah Mutala is a woman with a vision: the local church can lead the way in caring for orphans and break down the stigma associated with Aids. As the national women's co-ordinator for the Evangelical Fellowship of Zambia (EFZ), a long-standing Tearfund partner, Mrs Mutala has mobilised an army of volunteers. They visit the sick to bring comfort and practical help. Today, Mrs Mutala is with the volunteers in Josephine's house. As the visit nears its end, they sing a song together with a simple, uplifting message. Their voices are warm, rising in close harmonies.

'There's no-one, there's no-one like Jesus …'

The women weep when they pray.

'We call upon you father,' prays Mrs Mutala. 'You are the father to the orphans. You are the

God who answers prayers; the God who loves, the God who cares …'

Josephine is feeling better since their last visit. Then she was barely able to speak. Now the chest pain is less. But she's weak from lack of food.

'Since my husband died, life has been very difficult,' she says. 'When the children have no food, and the baby is sick, it makes me sad. The ladies from the church are the ones who usually take care of me.'

Their practical demonstration of God's love helps Josephine say:

'I know God is in control. He knows my situation; he's the hope I have. That's why even if I worry or struggle, I just look into God.'

There's no welfare system to help the poorest people in Zambia, but there are still school fees and rent to pay, books and school uniforms to buy. Increasingly it's the elderly, the grandparents and great-grandparents, who are left to pick up the pieces. The old watch the young die and are heartbroken and mystified. Aids killed 2.3 million people – 3,600 a day – in Africa last year, stealing a generation and decimating the workforce.

Aids has devastated Catherine's family. She lost four children last year, leaving seven grandchildren in her care. Two more of her daughters died this year. They were just about to get married. Her last daughter has been critically ill but is a little better now. Catherine, who is in her 60s, collapsed when her last son, Stephen, died.

'He was our breadwinner,' she says. 'He was supporting his family. So when he died it was a blow.'

Catherine is still so overwhelmed by grief she finds it hard to cry. But she weeps today when the women pray, deep cries of a raw grief.

The volunteers from the churches have been trained in counselling, thanks to a small Tearfund grant.

'I am encouraged by help from the church,' says Catherine. 'I am strengthened by their prayers when they comfort me.'

But it's not easy. Catherine and her husband, James, a carpenter, have become parents and providers all over again, at an age when they hoped their children would care for them – their only pension.

Maggie's husband died a year ago. Like Stephen, he was the breadwinner of the family.

'After my husband died, I used to get odd jobs like typing in an office,' Maggie says. 'Sometimes I'd help older ladies pound grain.'

But now Maggie is ill with TB, probably Aids related. She finds it hard to scratch a living for her and her four children. The little

money they have goes on essential medicine
for Maggie.

'These days I can't lift heavy things or do
hard jobs for long. When you get sick, your
work gets sick.'

Daily life becomes even harder. 'I struggle to
feed my children,' says Maggie. 'Sometimes I
know they'll end up having just one meal a day,
as young as they are. It feels bad seeing them
suffering.'

For Maggie and her family, Mrs Mutala and
the ladies from the local church are a lifeline.

'At least they come, the sisters, with their bag
of food and cooking oil,' says Maggie. 'It helps,
knowing they will come.'

But Maggie has another lifeline. Every morning, she makes a small fire outside her home
and boils a pot of water. She and her children
pray, asking God to come and help them.
Every day a small piece of meat or some veg-
etables appear in the pot. They don't know
who puts it there, but it proves to them that
God cares.

'Sometimes I feel I am lost, but then I think,
no, the Lord loves me,' Maggie says.

Here is faith that moves mountains.

Claudia, Maggie's eldest daughter, is 14 and
has learning difficulties. She introduced her
mother to the church. She starts singing a song
she learnt in Sunday school. She has a beautiful
voice.

'The Lord who is merciful, he has lifted me up from despair / Every day he is lifting me up . . .'

In some families, all the adults have died. We're in Lusaka, Zambia's capital, at Angela's house. When the volunteers from Tearfund partner EFZ arrive there are five children sitting on the floor, eating porridge from a shared bowl. There's barely enough food for one. Angela, the oldest at 15, isn't eating. She lies on the bed, half asleep. She says she's sick, but she just looks hungry. When Mrs Mutala asks Angela about this later, she shrugs it off.

'I can bear the pain of hunger. I want the others to eat.'

Mrs Mutala sits on the bed with Angela and puts her arm round her. They talk in hushed voices.

'I feel heartbroken when I remember how our mother cared for us,' says Angela. 'I miss her.'

There are the remnants of two families here. All four parents have died, leaving five children below the age of fourteen: Robert, Francis, Beatrice, Marita and four-year-old Munya. Their aunt Lina is the only adult left. She visits when she can. But the full burden of caring for the family has fallen on to Angela. Last year Angela was in grade five at school, but they threw her out because she couldn't pay. Her aunt went to plead, but they wouldn't take her back. Mrs Mutala asks Angela what gives her the strength to go on.

'Each morning I sit with the younger brothers and sisters and we pray,' she replies, breaking down in tears.

Angela goes from house to house looking for jobs. Sometimes they ask her to wash for them. They give her bread or meal or maybe 500 kwacha – about 10 pence. When they offer her food, she brings it home to her brothers and sisters.

The women have brought sweets as well as food. Robert, aged 14, has learning difficulties and can't unwrap his sweet, so his aunt does it for him. The future doesn't look bright. But Angela doesn't seem daunted.

'My dream is to get education,' she says. 'Then I will be able to take care of my brothers and sisters. I want them to have education too.'

After the visits, the volunteers sit and discuss what they have seen.

'When you go into the community, you are overwhelmed,' says Monica Williams.

'But we have been challenged by the word of God that it is *our* duty to look after people,' adds Cecilia Myunda.

The women go to extraordinary lengths. They hold women's meetings at church and appeal for clothes and food. Mary Soko arranged for 30 orphans to be cared for by the street children project where she works as an administrator. Ann Mukelabi, a teacher, has gained support in the schools.

'We speak out on behalf of those children who cannot afford to pay school fees,' she says. 'We plead with the authorities to give the families time to pay.'

Each teacher at her school contributes to a fund for the orphans. They raise awareness of the orphans' plight with parents. Local businesses are increasingly involved. Shoprite – a South African supermarket chain – has made donations and is planning more. EFZ's volunteers themselves are not wealthy. But they dip into their own pockets and raid their own kitchens for food to take with them on visits.

The problem is that Zambia is increasingly poor, still burdened by massive debt payments and harsh economic restructuring. There are already 12 million orphans in Africa, and many more to come. There is simply no way that charities or governments could provide for all their needs.

'Our government is perpetually looking to the donors,' says Mrs Mutala. 'But donors are not the whole answer. They cannot give love and support. We recognise that God has to move through the hearts of the Zambian people.'

A little goes a long way when it enables the local church to face problems like HIV/Aids in its own community.

Mrs Mutala urges the volunteers on.

'We are not going to have missionaries come and care for our own people. We are doing this as though Jesus Christ was here: we become his hands and his presence. Time is precious – this is the opportunity God has given us to make an impact. We look to the Lord.'

Perhaps this is the future for Africa: communities – and the church in particular – mobilised to deal with their own problems. Andrew Tomkins, Professor at the London Institute of Child Health and Tearfund board member, believes that Western governments and international agencies must respond with substantial aid.

'Education is vital in communities where there are many orphaned children,' he says. 'But agencies and institutions cannot provide the care and nurture that unparented children need. This is where the churches have a vital role to play. National Christians need our support as they are often the only providers of compassion and love for children living with the pain of being affected by HIV/Aids. Africa's affliction with Aids is like a dark night. But the inspirational work of people like these Zambian Christians shines out like bright stars.'

Taking more lives every year than the Kosovo, Sudan and Hurricane Mitch disasters together, HIV/Aids is Africa's biggest disaster, says Doug Balfour, Tearfund's General Director. He recently visited Tearfund partners working with HIV/Aids-affected people in four countries in southern Africa, finding many stories that echoed those of Josephine, Maggie, Catherine, Angela and Robert – and many 'bright stars'. The following is his personal response to the HIV/Aids crisis in Africa.

Clarina lives in Mozambique. Her home has holes in the wall and gaps in the roof. At 13 years old, she is the head of her family, with 2 younger brothers to support. Clarina's father developed HIV/Aids and died. Her mother remarried, but then she and her new husband died from HIV/Aids-related sickness. Her mother's extended family took in the older children, leaving Clarina and her brothers to fend for themselves. I look at Clarina and Melito – her smiling eight-year-old brother in a worn, ragged T-shirt – and ask how she copes.

'It's very difficult trying to live on our own,' she says. 'It's lonely, I need help, there are so many difficulties.'

But thankfully Clarina and her brothers are not alone. In addition to Agnes, their neighbour, they receive ongoing help from Kubatsirana, a local Christian HIV/Aids agency and Tearfund partner.

*Like the volunteers in Zambia, Kubatsirana's work-
ers come regularly to bring food, cook and teach
people like Clarina how to run a home – even in such
desperate circumstances. They're aiming to get
Clarina into school three days a week, which would
still leave her enough time to work to buy food.*

*Later that day, we visit Pastor Joaquim Mussirife
and his church members. He tells us that for 15
years he has been deeply challenged in his response
to the HIV/Aids crisis.*

*'Once we didn't dare touch people with
HIV/Aids. Now we know what to do,' he says.*

*He and his church started a school in 1996 for
children who have lost one or both parents because
the widows in the community could not afford to
buy school uniforms, books and pay examination
fees. Church members helped to build a 2-classroom
school that now holds 156 children, a third of whom
have no living parents. Each church family now
regularly contributes a small amount of money to
subsidise the voluntary teachers.*

*Kubatsirana offered five home-care workers, seven
youth educators, the church leadership and church
members places on an HIV/Aids training programme. The mothers in the church started to teach
the orphaned children how to sow. The church bought
a field and planted sunflowers to create income to support the expanding home-care work. And each church
member bought a little extra maize to give to poorer
families so they could plant on the church field.*

Compassion in action – linked to honest confrontation of the real issues of parenting, sexual behaviour and family planning, previously untouchable subjects in African culture – is having positive results in these communities.

As I reflect on these encounters in Mozambique and Zambia, I'm deeply impressed by two contrasting realisations: first, the tragedy of the HIV/Aids pandemic that is decimating the population of southern Africa; second, the realisation of hope, for it is the churches that are intimately involved in volunteering to care for these HIV/Aids sufferers and their families. The volunteers visit, bed-bath, cook, clean homes, bring food, befriend, teach hygiene, counsel and pray for and with these stigmatised, sick people.

This is the church being the hands and face of Jesus. This is Christ in each care-worker reaching out to those who are dying, sick and abandoned. This is the transformational church in the heart of the community, preaching faithfulness and abstinence, but loving HIV/Aids-affected people in practical, tangible ways.

As Tearfund's Director, I'm proud to be a Christian associated with these ordinary people doing an extraordinary work. Maybe this picture of the local church in action is nearer to God's intentions than the stained glass and respectable Sunday worship that we know so well.

But Africa's people living in poverty and HIV/Aids-affected communities need affordable, *accessible medical help to complement the love and care of these Christian care-workers. So I pray that some of the small amount of debt relief promised for southern Africa – and the rest that we are still praying and working for – will impact the people I met there. This, along with the generous gifts of Christians around the world, could help transform poor communities, bringing physical help as well as emotional and spiritual healing.*

I'm encouraged that Christians are having a significant effect on people suffering as a result of HIV/Aids – from the volunteers generously providing one-to-one care in Mozambique and Zambia to their UK brothers and sisters in Christ who continue to pray and give generously to help them.

The lesson is that we all have a part to play.

Some names in this article have been changed.

TELLING THE TRUTH

Jill Briscoe was born in Liverpool, England. She married Stuart Briscoe in 1958, and since then they have ministered together through their Telling the Truth media ministries and through presentations to conferences and mission organisations around the world. Jill has written or co-authored numerous articles and more than 40 books.

Briscoe Bulletin: United Flight 929

by Jill Briscoe

It was September 11 2001 and I was on United Flight 929 heading for Chicago and home. As the pilot began to dump fuel into the Atlantic, rudely waking the unsuspecting passengers in the cabin from a snooze, I looked over at my neighbour. We both raised our eyebrows.

'Now then', the captain announced over the intercom, 'we have a healthy aircraft.'

'Well, that's good!' I said.

But the cabin crew was suddenly far too busy for my liking. What were they doing? If the plane was healthy and the weather fine, why were we dumping fuel, and why were we unmistakably hearing the wheels being lowered? I looked at my watch. We were approximately three-and-a-half hours out of London's Heathrow airport. My husband had seen me off and stayed to minister in Northern Ireland, after four wonderful weeks of ministry together in Siberia and Russia.

'All airspace and borders have been closed in and out of the United States,' the pilot continued. 'We have been informed we have a national emergency on our hands and will be landing in 20 minutes at Gander airport in Newfoundland. I can't tell you any more until we are on the ground. Crew, prepare the cabin for landing.'

My seat companion was a young heart surgeon.

'I hope we aren't going to need you,' I said.

'So do I,' he replied with feeling.

'So, what do you think?' I asked him after a few stunned moments.

He shook his head, puzzled.

'Maybe a nuclear reactor?' he suggested.

'Taliban', I said.

I had just been in Russia, where the Taliban had featured heavily in the news and they came readily to mind as we debated what on earth could have caused such drastic measures. We couldn't figure out though why all the airspace and borders in the USA would have been closed if indeed the Taliban were terrorising people half a world away.

We and the 6,000 others in the 27 planes busily landing in Gander, Newfoundland (doubling the population), were left wondering and not a little apprehensive. Psalm 139:16 came readily to mind: 'All the days ordained for me were written in your book before one of them came to be.' 'Even September 11 2001 Lord', I murmured.

Along with the other 200 people on the plane, I began reading hastily the emergency landing instructions in the pocket in front of me. I experienced two things. First, a settled certainty that there was nowhere else in the whole wide world where I should be at this moment other than in this airplane seat, firmly buckled into the ordained will of God for me. '"Everyday", it says Lord. "Everyday". That includes September 11 as surely as it means all my yesterdays and all my tomorrows doesn't it?' *Yes*, said that still small voice in my soul. I recognised the whisper of his grace. Second, I knew a heady sense of anticipation for what-ever was ahead. Of course, none of us in the skies had an inkling of the size and shape of the horrific events that had unfolded in Washington and Manhattan an hour or so after we were airborne. But God was good to give me 30 saving minutes before landing to check my theology and make sure it was securely in place before we were informed of the horrific things that had happened.

What did I believe? That God was in control even when I wasn't? Yes! That nothing could happen to his children apart from his permissive will? Yes! That God was good – all the time, even when things were bad? Yes! That I and other Jesus lovers and glory givers on that plane had a colossal advantage over those who had no high tower for their soul to run into; no good shepherd to calm their beating hearts, hush their fears and remind them that if the very worst was to happen, the very best was yet to come? Yes!

Still in our seats 12 hours later, waiting for processing by the Canadian authorities before leaving our luggage on the plane and being driven 30 miles to the Salvation Army church in Gambo, Newfoundland (I'd always wanted to go to Gambo!), I had reason enough to settle into 6 days of 'God experiences'. If I really believed what I believed, this would be an unprecedented opportunity to do what Stuart and I had just been training pastors, leaders and missionaries all over Russia to do: establish a presence, gain credibility, and speak for Christ in the situation, to anyone who would listen.

Well, I had established a presence by getting on my flight at Heathrow! There was no need to take the risks of countless missionaries worldwide, putting themselves intentionally into harm's way for the sake of Christ and his Kingdom. My 'village' or 'people group' was composed of 200 passengers and crew from many different cultures and countries, and I was firmly established among them.

I needed to gain credibility. How? I knew the answer to that one – by my reactions to the situations we found ourselves in and my loving response to those around me. Immediately, I faced my first test. All meals, save breakfast and emergency rations, had been eaten, so the crew announced they would wait for four hours before feeding us the food they had left as they had no idea how long we would be shut up on the plane. My mind flew to my purse, where I had a packet of biscuits (read 'cookies'). A struggle ensued. *I'll wait till everyone's asleep*, I thought, *and then nibble them scrumptiously*! I was immediately horrified at myself. *Well, that's a great way to begin to gain credibility*, I lectured my soul. Any fancy ideas I had had of rising to the occasion for Jesus disappeared!

God helped me to do a little bit better as the days went by. Sleeping on a pew or an army cot may sound like fun for a night, but it gets old after six – even though I had the joy of a mattress for three nights! Sitting around on church chairs for 12 hours a day, or queuing up for one of the 3 phones shared among some 200 people for far too long, only to hear the engaged signal, adds up to a lot of frustration! It was time to take spiritual advantage of the situation and seize the day. I set about my unexpected task to gain quick access to the hearts and minds of the people God had brought into my life for this short time. How to start?

I prayed – all the time. I smiled – all the time – at everybody! I began touching an arm or a shoulder day by daily day and asking simply, 'How are you doing?' From the very first day people responded. In fact, one girl asked me 'What on earth have you got to smile about?' I told her!

I found myself more excited than I could imagine, with a growing consciousness of the importance of every hour and especially meal times at the long Salvation Army tables.

We were served by Salvation Army staff whose mercy gift shouted louder than words to all of us. 'We lucked out being here,' a passenger commented. 'I don't know why they have been so giving and kind to us.' I told him!

Which people should I sit with Lord? I prayed as breakfast, lunch and dinner came along. Meal after meal I found God had prepared hearts around me. Some needed a challenge or a provoking thought, others assurance or comfort, a child a story or a game of cards. I was stretched as others debated deep and difficult things. I tried to put as many links on the chain of salvation as I could, believing others would add theirs in the days ahead. It turned out to be one of the most challenging, frustrating, self-revealing, exciting, productive, God-shadowed weeks of my life!

I certainly didn't win every argument about the character of God (How could a good God let this happen?) or the wisdom of God (Why did he 'make' hunger in the first place?). Neither were there necessarily receptive ears to my biblical perspectives (this is God's world and he wants it back). But I got agreement that we were a thankful planeload of people. Thankful to be alive and safe, and, that as far as the authorities could tell, there were no known terrorists or their associates aboard as some feared. They were a great bunch of people too. We had a wonderful captain and crew and lots of passengers who rose to the occasion to keep our spirits up or calm things down when people's patience frayed. We even had a musician who had been heading to Nashville sing for us (and with us) for six days. I discovered the best – and worst – of people comes out in such times. But I was also thankful for the chance to put some of the faith I talk and write about so easily to work in a difficult setting.

I thought a lot about the prayer I had requested from the pulpit of our church on the eve of this trip to England, Siberia, Russia and – as it turned out – Newfoundland! I had asked specially for prayers for our travelling safely on the roads and in the car. We had learned the previous month that the flight we would be taking into Irkutsk had crashed, killing all on board. The captain could not get landing permission from the drunken air traffic controller and, after circling the airport for a while, ran out of fuel and crashed. I thought about the four-hour trip on Russian roads that should have been easy, but took twelve hours, with many adventures along the way. I had no doubt whatsoever that our loving friends and family had done sterling battle on their knees, for the devil, as we know, is a murderer from the beginning.

*   *   *

As we recover from the incredible events of September 11 and regroup spiritually for what is around the corner of tomorrow, I am encouraged by my own small experience. He waits with our future in his hands and it will be all right. Whatever the whatever and whenever the whenever, God is God enough. Sadder and wiser may we Americans return to our God and give ourselves with greater urgency to the most important and necessary things in life.

Jesus said, 'As long as it is day, we must do the work of him who sent me. Night is coming, when no one can work' (John 9:4). The sun is still in the sky, but perhaps it is setting and we must be about our father's business. This is not a 'may be', but a 'must be'. Paul catches the urgency in Romans 10 and 1 Corinthians 7:29.

The time is short (the days are evil). From now on:

- Those who have wives should live as if they had none;
- Those who mourn as if they did not;
- Those who are happy as if they were not;
- Those who use the things of the world as if not engrossed in them.

This world in its present form is passing away. And the writer to the Hebrews says, 'Once more I will shake not only the earth but also the heavens' (12:26). The words 'once more' indicate the removing of what can be shaken – that is, created things. So that what cannot be shaken may remain.

> Therefore, since we are receiving a kingdom that cannot be shaken, let us be thankful, and so worship God acceptably with reverence and awe, for our 'God is a consuming fire' (Hebrews 12:28).

So let's be thankful and worship God.

SEND THE LIGHT LTD

Keith Danby is Chief Executive of Send The Light Ltd, Europe's leading supplier of English language Christian books, gifts, music, software and video products. The company has close links with Operation Mobilisation, giving a percentage of its profits to the work of OM India.

Why Have I Made You Indian?

by Keith Danby

Spring 1990 : Carlisle, England

It was a fine Saturday morning and, for a change, it was not overcast or raining. We had moved to the north of England to live in the Cumbrian border City of Carlisle in the summer of 1989 and, although it was less than a year ago, it now seemed like we had lived here all our lives. I had wakened early and had been for my run along the Eden river-bank, a vital part of my weekend routine, had showered and was now enjoying my first cup of coffee – always the best one of the day! I was savouring a few moments' quiet when I heard the doorbell ring. The rest of the family were in various stages of wakefulness, so my immediate thought was that the caller must be, either the postman, delivering a package too big for the letter-box, or a friend of one of my two girls eager to start their play-filled day early. It was, to my surprise, neither, but my friend Stephen, – Dr Stephen Alfred, to be correct.

I was pleased to see Stephen – he had become
one of my closest friends, since moving to the
area. He was a very dedicated surgeon and
worked long hours at the hospital, which
meant we usually only met at church or in the
evenings, after all his ward rounds were completed. He was post-fellowship registrar at The
Cumberland Infirmary – Carlisle's main hospital – a post he had taken up in the autumn of
1989. It was also widely predicted that he
would be the next surgical consultant, when Mr
Martin Lyons, the highly respected incumbent,
retired in a few years' time.

Stephen and I, were an unlikely match as
friends: he had no interest in business or sport,
rarely had time to read and had virtually no
interest in music, especially contemporary. Our
two anchor points were our Christian faith and
India. Stephen was Indian and had moved to
the UK to train as a surgeon. I visited India at
least twice a year in connection with my work
with Send the Light and Operation Mobilisation, two Christian charities.

Stephen and I also had a mutual friend who
took a special interest in our lives. I first met
Bill Thompson in September 1987, when I
spoke at his church. It happened to be my very
first weekend with Operation Mobilisation and
I was asked to speak at the service because the
person scheduled to be there had been taken ill.
It was an OM India orientation meeting and my

qualification for speaking, was, it seemed, that I just happened to be free! Up to that time I had never been to India, nor had I ever spoken at an OM meeting, so I felt as if I was being pushed in at the deep end. My lasting memory of the occasion was seeing Bill for the first time. I stepped nervously into the pulpit, and saw a tall man in a dark blue suit, white shirt and red tie sitting a few rows from the front holding an enormous Bible. It seemed he was staring right at me. I do not remember much about the sermon but I do recall the fright I had when I noticed Bill walking straight towards me as I lifted my head and opened my eyes after the closing prayer! 'My name is Bill Thompson', he said, 'and I would like to invite you to my home for tea'. Before I could object, I found myself heading in the direction of his home, which was close to the church.

Looking back now, some 15 years later, I can thank God for what, at the time, seemed an untimely and rather insensitive telephone call from George Verwer requesting that I speak at that unusual meeting. Bill became my spiritual overseer. He has prayed for me every day from that first encounter and has called me on the telephone every month for my 'spiritual health check-up'. He is always direct and honest with questions: 'How am I doing?' 'What am I reading'? 'What am I preaching on?' 'How much time am I spending away from home?' 'How is the family doing?' 'What are the issues I am struggling with at work?' Bill became the source of sound advice and encouragement, but more than anything else he became like a father to me, always ready to be a listening ear and someone with whom I felt I could share even my most confidential thoughts. I was one of Bill's boys! Bill knew men like me all around the world and he kept in touch with each of them regularly. Stephen was also one of Bill's boys.

Bill had himself lived in India for over 20 years directing the work of Gospel Literature Outreach in Bombay. He was a close friend of the Alfred family and had watched Stephen grow up as a child, following his developments very closely. When Stephen was relocating to Carlisle, Bill contacted me to make sure I looked out for him. Stephen, of course, also had instructions from Bill, to look out for me!

As Stephen and I sat opposite each other at the kitchen table I could see that this was no ordinary visit, and over coffee I began to understand the reason why. Stephen had already had breakfast, been to the hospital and had completed a ward round. I had not seen him for several weeks as I had been away on business, so we caught up on the small talk. I then gently steered the conversation towards what was really on his mind. He sat perfectly still, his face impassive, showing no emotion – I could see why he was a surgeon. There was that expectant pause when you know that something important is about to be said and your mind focuses on the statement about to be made. I had to try to control my mind which was racing ahead. Had someone died – his father or mother or one of his sisters? Had something gone wrong with one of his surgical procedures at the hospital? Had he met someone, fallen in love and was about to get married?

I would never have been able to predict his opening sentence. He looked me straight in the eye and said, 'Last night God spoke to me'.

I sat in stunned silence, not because I did not believe that God spoke to people any more, or that the God of miracles could not still perform the unusual, but because having worked in an interdenominational organisation for several years I had heard similar comments on many occasions. But hearing this from Stephen was a shock! He was an evangelical; from an ultra-conservative Indian Brethren background. I concluded that something dramatic must have happened. I sat pensively and silently for a few moments wondering what to say and how I should respond. Then I looked at him and said, 'What do you think this means, Stephen?'

With great thoughtfulness, he began to tell me some of his family background. His mother and father were still alive and lived in Thane, a city with a population of three million, that adjoins Bombay, which itself has a population of 20 million. His parents were both deeply committed Christians: his father was an elder in a small Brethren church; his mother a quiet caring person given to warm loving hospitality. There were three children and Stephen, being the oldest son, had a special place in the family in accordance with Indian tradition. His two sisters, Margaret and Lydia, were both married and were also very active in their faith.

Stephen went on to describe his reaction to a telephone call from his youngest sister, Lydia, in which she had told him that she and her husband, Raghu, were going into full-time Christian service in Siliguri, to work mainly with Nepalese village people. He had been irritated and unsympathetic and had tried to convince her that she should not give up her good job and her career – 'there were other people who could do this type of work', he had told her firmly. One year earlier, in 1987, his other sister, Margaret, along with her husband, Sam, had gone to work in remote villages in Dehra Dun northern India, doing evangelism, community projects and church planting.

'For several years, instead of being proud of what my sisters were doing, I have felt very uncomfortable' Stephen continued. 'Instead of being encouraging I was somewhat cynical. But last night I could not escape the fact that God was speaking directly to me. I felt he was asking me, "Why have I made you Indian?" India is a land of almost a billion people, where over 60 per cent live in abject poverty: 90 per cent of the population are Hindu, 6 per cent are Muslim, 2 per cent belong to other world religions such as Buddhism but only 2 per cent are Christian. I am one of those 2 per cent. None of us can influence where we are born: that is God's ultimate choice. Therefore, surely there is a purpose in why God has made me an Indian?

'I believe God also asked me, "Why have I made you good?" By his grace he blesses each of us with natural talents and gifting. Why am I a doctor? For most of my life, I have wanted to do nothing else other than to study medicine and to become a doctor. In India for a Christian to train as a doctor it is particularly difficult. The universities and medical schools mainly cater for Hindu students with places reserved for scholarship students and fee-paying students. There is also a small allocation of places for Muslims, but it is very difficult for Christians, even if their parents have the resources to pay. Of course, everyone has to sit an entrance examination and the authorities have to offer places to students with the very highest grades. I managed to get a place on merit. Now I am in the UK and I am one of a handful of doctors that have been part of a project to pioneer keyhole surgery in the UK. I am heading for a senior post at The Cumberland Infirmary and I am still only in my early 30s. I sensed God ask me, "Why have I made you good?"

'When I left India to come to the UK, I vowed to myself that I would not return to India except to visit my family or for a holiday. India is a wonderful country, but there is so much poverty and corruption. The system is governed by the bribe – without it very little happens. I was tired of this and resented it so much that I resolved not to return. I was deserting my own people! I was turning my back on the India I loved! Last night I felt God was asking me, "Why have you deserted your own people?"'

As I listened intently to Stephen's story, I felt like I was watching a scene similar to that of Moses at the burning bush! Should I take off my shoes because this was holy ground? God was working in Stephen's life and this was a sacred and precious moment. 'Stephen', I said somewhat hesitantly, 'it seems obvious to me that you are going back to India!'

Summer 1998 : North Carolina, USA

There were four of us waiting in the reception area of the joint offices of Samaritan's Purse and World-wide Medical Mission in Boone, North

Carolina. We had each funded our own tickets. David Vardy and I had flown in from the UK, Ed Long from Mount Pleasant, Michigan, and Stephen from India. We were waiting to see Robert Bell, the Vice President of Ministry and right-hand man to Franklin Graham, the President of the two organisations. I could not work out whether this was the smartest thing we had done in the last five years or the most reckless. During the car journey from the airport to the offices we had rehearsed our strategy several times. David, who was the CEO of the Billy Graham Evangelistic Association in the UK, had impressed upon us several times that we would have only one chance to get this right. Samaritan's Purse is involved in relief and mission projects all around the world and has a multi-million dollar budget, but it has so many applications for aid it has to turn down 99.9 per cent. I could not recall ever being so nervous!

We were welcomed into a spacious office and offered refreshments. Robert Bell was warm and friendly, but as we were an hour late he got right down to business after a few introductions. David had explained to us that he had been the Bell of 'Cissco Bell' one of the largest food distribution companies in the States. After selling his share of the business, he had come to help Franklin Graham run these two organisations, and it did not take us long to work out that he was a very astute business-man.

We had worked out our plan carefully. David was to make the brief introductions and then he would hand over to Stephen. Stephen would tell the story of how his vision for the hospital first came about, how it became a real-ity and how the hospital now functions from day to day. He would hand over to me and I would make the request for help. But before we had the chance to compose ourselves, Robert started things rolling: 'Now gentlemen, how can I help you?'

Stephen took a deep breath and began his story; 'In 1990 I believe God called me back to India to work with my own people. At the time, I had a position of a senior medical officer at The Cumberland Infirmary in Carlisle in the UK. With the help of some friends we set up a charity in the UK, which we called the Thane Trust. Thane is a city of three million people next to Bombay, where I was brought up. The plan was that I would return to India and we would try to start a mission hospital. I would be a 'tent maker' – working in a number of hospitals for a salary alongside the mission hos-pital project for free. Even before I returned to India I was offered a job at the JK Hospital, which is one of the best hospitals in the region. Patients I treat at this hospital are charged the highest rates for private medical care and I receive a good salary as a result of this, which helps me to support my wife, Claire, and our two young boys, Joshua and Benjamin.

'By the grace and provision of God, today we have a 35-bed hospital, which is called the Bethany Hospital, where we handle a wide range of patients. Our policy is to charge those who can afford to pay the going rate and those who cannot afford to pay get free or subsidised care, depending on their circumstances. We try to balance it roughly between 50 per cent fee paying and 50 per cent free or subsidised. I work in the JK Hospital and the other small hospitals, mainly in the morning, and then at the Bethany Hospital in the afternoon and late evening. I also hold an early evening clinic in some small consulting rooms, which I rent on Gokhale Road, close to Thane railway station. Often the evening clinic acts as a feeder to the Bethany Hospital.'

Robert Bell listened carefully to Stephen's concise but moving account. Then he looked at me and began to ask a number of questions in rapid succession.

'You have bought some land, is that right?'

'Yes', I replied.

'Is it paid for?' Bell asked.

'Yes', I replied again.

'Are there any outstanding loans?' Bell continued.

'There are no outstanding loans' I stated.

Bell quickly moved onto his next set of questions. 'You have built a 35-bed hospital?'

I nodded my head. 'Yes'.

'Is it paid for?' he repeated.

'Yes, it is paid for' I replied.

He pressed me still further. 'Are there any outstanding loans?'

'There are no outstanding loans' I responded again.

Bell finally moved to his next series of questions. 'Have you equipped the hospital?'

'Yes, we have equipped the hospital'.

'Is it paid for?'

'Yes, it is all paid for'.

Without missing a beat, he asked again, 'Are there any outstanding loans?' Not wishing to break the rhythm, I said in quick response, 'No, there are no outstanding loans'.

Bell broke off for a moment and said, 'This is amazing – tell me, how did you do this?'

I looked across to Stephen as if to give him the cue. Stephen began to fill in the background and told Bell the story of what happened after our Saturday morning meeting, in my home back in the spring of 1990. 'We brought together a handful of men from the north of England I had got to know during my time there – there were five in total. We formed a UK charity, which we called the Thane Trust. We met together to pray and dream about what might be. I was increasingly convinced that

God was calling me back to India to start a hospital, which would essentially be used to help the poorest of the poor. I notified the Carlisle hospital, where I worked at the time, of my intention to return to India and we came to an amicable agreement on the notice period, which was still quite uncertain.'

I interrupted Stephen, to mention another important development, as well as to give him a break, as I could see how nervous he was. 'Around this time Stephen met Claire, a nurse training in the same hospital', I continued. 'Claire was from Wylam, a small town in Northumberland, and she chose Carlisle because it was only about 40 miles away from her home. On her first week in the surgical ward she assisted Stephen in the operating theatre. She had heard from other nurses of how difficult it could be in theatre, as sometimes the surgeons could be quite gruff! Stephen, however, was different from what she expected; during the procedures he quietly hummed a hymn or worship song, which of course she recognised. At the end of the session, Claire plucked up the courage to ask him if he was a Christian. They met again at the hospital's Christian Fellowship, which Stephen had recently started, and the relationship developed from there.'

'The big issue for us', Stephen said as he picked up the story, 'was India! Claire had not visited India and I felt compelled to move back there. After some wise counsel from some close friends, including Bill Thompson and his wife, Dorothy, it was agreed that we should visit India together for three weeks. This would give me chance to seek out the possibility of attachments at some hospitals in the area, firm up my contact at the JK Hospital and make some initial plans for my return. Whilst there, I also asked some of my closest friends in India to be part of an accountability group and to help me form an Indian charitable foundation, which would become the organisation to conduct the ministry from. We decided to call this the Bethany Trust.

'This trip would also expose Claire to life in India and allow her to see how she would cope with the huge culture shock. This was an incredibly important time in our lives and many of our close friends committed to pray for us both daily. My parents were a great help as they immediately took Claire into their home and made her feel loved and wanted. At the end of the holiday we both returned excited about how well the trip had gone and with a real sense that God had confirmed his calling on both of our lives and the new ministry in India.

'A great deal happened in a very short time. We set a date to be married on April 11 1992 and after a few days' honeymoon in the English Lake District we moved to live in India.'

'Meanwhile, like the events you read about in missionary biographies, people heard about the project and offers of help, support and equipment began to come in. Among the things we were to have shipped to India with our possessions was an operating table donated by the South Shields Hospital, where I had worked for a period.

'Once in India, the momentum continued and money was provided for me to set up a small clinic in a busy area next to Thane railway station for evening clinics. Two of the trustees from the UK visited India on a regular basis as part of their work, so a close working relationship was quickly established between the UK and Indian trustees.

'Thane was a rapidly developing area, with an emerging middle-class population and a lot of housing development, mainly multi-storey apartment blocks, under construction. I made contact with a developer and I was able to secure a site to build a hospital in the Pokhran district, at a very attractive price.'

Again, I interrupted. 'This was the point at which the UK trustees, in particular, had to make some serious decisions. The signing of a contract to purchase land, and then to build a hospital, meant there would be no way back. This was for real! Affirmed by what had remarkably taken place so far, and after much prayer, we agreed unanimously to take the next steps. However, we each agreed that this was a project that had three phases to it. Stage one, was the purchase of the land. Stage two, was the building of the hospital. Stage three, was the equipping of the hospital. We also agreed that we would not move on to the next stage until God had provided the resources to complete the current phase.

'There were occasions when we felt God to be our only hope. He had to be our great deliverer. Stephen would telephone the UK to say that the developer wanted his next payment, but invariably there would be insufficient funds in the bank. However, on every occasion, unsolicited gifts came in, and covered what was needed.'

Robert Bell had sat silently, listening to every word. Then, with a sincere look of amazement, he asked, 'Why do you need our help?'

There was a moment of quiet. I looked at Stephen, unsure who should speak next, and then I said, 'We have taken the project as far as we can. I am an administrator and Stephen is a surgeon, and we did not realise just what was involved in setting up and running a hospital.'

Stephen went on to explain that he did not realise how important it was to have an ICU (intensive care unit) in a hospital. He explained that there were times when he had been conducting a serious procedure, often in the middle of the night, when complications had developed and the patient had needed to be transferred to a hospital with an ICU faculty. For any patient this is a difficult process. However, in India, it is usually a life-threatening exercise because of the perilous roads and vehicles. This had forced us to realise that we need an ICU ward at Bethany Hospital.

Robert Bell looked to me and asked, 'Do you have any idea how much it costs to set up an ICU ward in a hospital?'

'$40,000 per bed', I replied hesitantly.

'How many beds are you hoping for?' Bell asked.

'Four beds' Stephen replied.

Again there was a pause. 'It will cost at least $200,000 for a four bed unit, plus all the costs of surveying and installation', Bell stated. He looked thoughtful for a moment. The seconds seemed like hours. *This is not looking very hopeful*, I thought to myself.

Then Bell looked up and said to Stephen, 'I think we can help!' 'We will have to send over a medical team to survey the hospital and assess its suitability. If this goes well, we will source all the equipment in the USA and have it shipped to India. We will need to allocate $250,000 for this element of the project, to be on the safe side. We will then need to send over a team of technicians to install the equipment and commission it and, finally, we will need to send some medical teams over to train your people in how to use the equipment. The total cost of all of this is likely to be in the region of $400,000. We will do this through WMM, but you need to realise I am only one member of the World Medical Mission board, and Franklin Graham will have to approve it. However, the application will go with my recommendation. Now gentlemen, would you like some lunch?'

Autumn 2001 : Thane, India

As I walk around the hospital I am very conscious of how far we have come in the past ten years. Max Lucado, the best-selling author and speaker says, 'We should never underestimate the power of a seed'. The hospital is a testimony to this statement.

There are people everywhere. Nurses and medical staff are moving swiftly about their tasks. There are sick people waiting their turn to see a doctor or a nurse. The hospital is running at full capacity: all the beds are occupied. Family and friends seek to offer comfort and support. Many will have travelled for days, some on foot, to get to the hospital and it is not unusual for them to sleep on a bench or bed-roll at the end of the patient's bed for the whole of their stay. Although the wards are crowded there is a respectful silence.

Observing the reactions on the faces of the patients and the expression on Dr Alfred's face, as he goes about his daily ward rounds, I am reminded forcefully, once again, that this is no ordinary hospital. The staff and the patients have so much respect for Stephen's hard work, dedication and care. He treats each of his patients with respect and dignity. This is clearly, not just a job – it is a calling. Stephen goes about his tasks seeking each day to serve Christ and to show his love to those in his care, regardless of whether they are fee-paying or subsidised patients.

When the hospital was originally constructed it had two upper floors for the medical facility and a ground floor, where all the laundry was done. On Sundays this area is set out as a church, with chairs and a portable pulpit. The hospital has now had two additional floors built and there are plans to enclose the ground floor and use it to accommodate the reception and waiting area.

There are always several volunteers, from the USA, UK and Europe working at the hospital for a few weeks or months, often supported and encouraged by their church. This gives them an opportunity of short-term exposure to a different type of mission work. They are mainly young people, who frequently undertake the tasks that the doctors and nurses just do not have time for, such as giving post-operative

patients exercise, even if it is only walking them
to the end of the corridor. Sometimes just
simply sitting beside the beds and offering company and comfort is a tremendous help to the
patients. There are always a number of simple
domestic tasks to do each day, like folding the
laundry. Having willing hands is of great benefit.

I am also amazed at the wide range of spe-
cialist facilities the hospital has now. It is no
longer a small hospital with around 30 beds, a
small X-ray room and an operating theatre.
Now, it is an official project adopted by
Samaritan's Purse and the World Medical
Mission and has 50 beds including a 6-bed ICU,
a 4-bed neo–natal unit and fully equipped opti-
cal and dental units. I am surprised to see a
well-stocked pharmacy unit, and wonder when
this sprung into being! As I move through each
of these areas, I don't just see medical equipment and facilities, but the evidence of faith
and prayer. I recall the cheques, large and
small, from people, many of whom I will never
meet to thank personally, realising they will
never have chance to see the hospital for themselves.

I remember the many flights to India when
my baggage was filled, not with my clothes and
presents for my Indian friends, but with medical
equipment, collected from around the world. I
recall also the many telephone calls to various

airlines pleading for permission for yet another excess baggage allowance, in the hope that some day the equipment might save someone's life. I particularly remember bringing a diathermy machine all the way from the USA. This machine was a vital piece of equipment for the hospital because it uses electronic currents to produce heat in the deeper tissues of the body, thereby stopping bleeding and often saving a patient's life. When I agreed to bring it to the UK and then on to India I did not imagine it would be so big. It was so heavy it took two people to lift it into my car. Remarkably, I managed to clear it through American Airlines, KLM and even past the chief customs officer in Bombay Airport, who was clearly a Hindu, all without too much difficulty.

I cannot forget my friend Bill Thompson, who was one of the first people to recognise that Stephen was indeed a special Indian, gifted and anointed by God for an important task. My mind is filled with the sense of privilege: this has been one of the most exciting and most rewarding things I have ever been involved in. I also feel a sense of shame when I remember the times I doubted and lacked the faith to see God do the seemingly impossible. I recall the times when I felt like Abraham must have felt when he was on Mount Moriah. He was seeking to do what God had told him to do, even though it did not seem to make sense to him.

The Bethany Hospital is a testimony of God's gracious calling of a man and his wife who were willing to be obedient and to move into the unknown, learning to trust with each new day and with each fresh demonstration of divine providence, that God does not make mistakes and that he keeps his promises.

I am reminded of what Philip Yancey wrote in his book, *Reaching for the Invisible God*, describing the work of the Holy Spirit in the life of the individual, he asks the question, 'Are you filled with the Spirit?' He goes on to make the conjecture;

'If you asked the apostle Paul such a question, he would likely respond by listing qualities that the Spirit produces: love, joy, peace, goodness, etc. Do you have those qualities? And do you express God's love for others? Each of Paul's letters ends with a call to practical acts of love and service: prayer, sharing with the needy, comforting the sick, hospitality, humility. We dare not devalue the 'ordinary' – actually, most extraordinary – work of God making himself at home in our lives. These are the marks of the Spirit-filled life, signs of the invisible made manifest in our visible world.'

When I see Stephen in the hospital or enjoy the warmth of the hospitality offered by Claire in their home, I see examples of the Spirit-filled life and see clear evidence of the love of God shed abroad in their hearts.

The hospital is a testimony to many individuals, churches, Christian charities and foundations who have recognised a work of God and have been willing to support it prayerfully and practically even when it seemed to be only a seed planted in the ground.

Finally, I think back to that Saturday morning and a young doctor who said 'Last night God spoke to me and asked me, ' "Why have I made you Indian?" '

OM INDIA

Operation Mobilisation works in more than 80 countries, motivating and equipping people to share God's love with people all over the world. OM seeks to help plant and strengthen churches, especially in areas of the world where Christ is least known.

India Travels: A Brief Journal
July 23 – August 4 2001

by Tony Sargent

The reason for this trip was to attend the biannual board meeting of Operation Mobilisation India, the largest group within OM International, whose work I have helped to direct for over 20 years. I was also to spend time with consultant surgeon Stephen Alfred of Bethany Hospital, Thane, Bombay. Interviews with individual Indians and interaction with relief and evangelistic groups will also have advantageous spin-off for the International Christian College, Glasgow. Before leaving the UK I kept a preaching engagement on the south coast.

Monday July 23

I leave Bournemouth on the 5.00 a.m. coach to
Heathrow and eventually benefit from a very
efficient KLM shuttle service to the Continent.
I am able to do some phoning before leaving
for Amsterdam and then get some work done
during the two-hour stopover. I reflect on yesterday at Lansdowne Baptist Church and am
so grateful for the warmth of welcome, as ever.
I can't believe my contact with this church
now goes back 30 years. I have been back
every year for so many of them. It seemed
right to preach from two psalms highlighting
the king on Zion (Psalm 2) and the citizens of
Zion (Psalm 84); the latter is a fantastic psalm
that gave an opportunity to preach on mission.
We concluded with a verse from Prince
Charles's favourite hymn, 'Saviour if of Zion's
City I through grace a member am'. What a
privilege!

Today I start to read two books: a new one
called *Evangelicalism Divided* by Iain Murray,
with a lot of references to Martyn Lloyd Jones;
also a book by one of the great Pentecostal
theologians of this century, Gordon Fee, a fascinating book on reading the Bible with the help
of the Spirit. I determine in my travels to get
back to consistent writing, having put this on
one side during my last year at Worthing Tab
and my first three years in Glasgow.

[On board]: I spend a couple of hours writing up e-mails, which I hope to send off when I get to India. It is not always easy to get a server to achieve this. There is a 'loss' of five hours as we fly into the night, which makes this a short day. One recoups the benefit on the return programme. KLM give good service – after an early 5.00 a.m. start from Bournemouth to Heathrow, I get aboard the flight to Amsterdam then wait a couple of hours for a connecting flight to Bombay. My mobile enables some contact both with my office and a variety of folk I need to call.

Tuesday July 24

I arrive in Bombay International at 3.00 a.m., not exactly a civilised time. Willie, my taxi friend, is as ever efficient and meets me to pass on internal tickets that I will need for the next few days and to take me over to the domestic airport. There is no time for a few hours' stopover at the local airport hotel. The flight for Ahmedabad leaves at 5.30 a.m. and we have but 90 minutes. By 7.00 a.m. I find myself in this 'Manchester' of India and am met by a squad of Omers plus part of the Matthews family, armed with the usual floral bouquet (what to do with them in the aftermath always puzzles me). The city is dirty and undisciplined – I

see no improvement over the 20 years or so I
have stayed here – though the line has to be
drawn with the airport. Why cattle, camels,
buffalo, pigs – not to mention dogs – are
allowed to roam freely is a puzzle. I imagine
most would prefer the green fields and grasses
of the countryside. The pollution hits one a
mile away, good for neither human nor beast.
Some of the animals are pathetic, such as the little donkey that flopped down exhausted from
the heat on the intersection of the main road
with the lane leading off to the Matthews'
home. Freedom for animals to roam where
they want may be part of Hinduism but in town
it is a colossal disadvantage. Presumably the
local people take some religious satisfaction in
feeding the cows, sacred to Hindus. The other
animals seem to live by scavenging.

This is monsoon season: I left the relatively
cold wet city of Glasgow for the warm wet city
of Ahmedabad. When it rains it really rains –
similar to standing under a shower, not
unpleasant – but you soon dry out. But the latter is not so easily achieved if you are living in
one of the slum dwellings that proliferate by
the sides of the roads and sometimes go back
many hundred yards in little alleys that run
with water mixed with foul refuse.

The Matthews' house is large and well kept –
a bargain investment of yesteryear. It is
positioned about 400 yards from the OM base.

'My' room is well prepared and I am glad to crash out after a shower. It has been an exhausting weekend with no more than 4 hours' sleep in 36. I don't usually feel so weary. I felt a loss of nervous energy when preaching and guess this is a contributory factor. I doze on and off for six hours, then spend the rest of the afternoon and evening catching up on news from the Matthews. I am to leave at 6.30 a.m. tomorrow for my journey to Kutch.

Wednesday July 25

A main reason for visiting Gujurat is to go directly to the areas most affected by the January earthquake. Not that Ahmedabad remained unscathed – many people died and buildings collapsed – but the damage is not so obvious; six months have elapsed and a good deal of repair work has been done. Rowena tells me how scary it was, the morning incident impressed indelibly on her memory. Her mother had a phone call from the earthquake area by coincidence. Her caller put the phone down having mentioned the building she phoned from was swaying. Within a couple of minutes the Matthews and all Ahmedabad had the same experience.

Throughout the state tens of thousands died. Whole villages, I was told, were devastated.

OM, with other larger organisations, made a world-wide appeal. I backed this in the UK. Large sums of money were given and I felt a duty to see how at least some of this was being spent and how OM, not known as a relief unit generally, was coping.

The two-hour journey I anticipated to the epicentre turned out to be over six hours, and though the hired vehicle was comfortable enough and well driven, the intense heat at times made the journey taxing. I kept drifting into a doze, which is neither refreshing nor relaxing. Between the dozing was conversation with young OMers. But none of them were genned up on the relief programme. As we got into the area of severe tremor we saw buildings with cracks and occasionally the driver was compelled to use hastily constructed bridges running parallel to the ones rendered useless. Eventually we reached Gandhidham, where my friend of long standing, Shaji, and his wife, Bina, were waiting to greet me from the veranda of their rented house.

Shaji headed up the Good Samaritan ministry in Calcutta and has several years of experience of working in urban deprivation. He achieved amazing advances in the slums, forfeiting completing his graduate work in order to give pioneer leadership to what was then a completely new ministry for OM. Because of his experience gained down the

years and his known integrity, OM asked Shaji
to cross the subcontinent and move to the
earthquake-affected area. This creates great
hardship for Bina. She comes from south India
and had a close relationship with Rita, the co-
leader of the Calcutta work's wife. Moving to
west India means exchanging one culture for
another and creates language problems. Bina
speaks no Gujurati, has two small children and
finds herself alone quite often, as Shaji has to
travel widely. But she is a brave as well as a
beautiful lass, and doubtless will settle. To the
loneliness is added the unwelcome presence of
swarms of flies. The place is infested with
them. Add to that the incredible heat in the
summer (no insulation from the roof) and
the mosquitoes at night, and you don't have
the best scenario for bringing up two young
children.

It is now two in the afternoon. Perspiration
drips from me. A cold or at least cool shower is
welcome, as is some food. Then Shaji suggests I
go his office, meet other leaders from non-govern-
ment organisations working in conjunction with
OM, and set off to see one of the villages. We have
ruled out returning the same night to Ahmedabad,
which was my original intention. I am offered a
room in a hotel but prefer to sleep on the floor in
Shaji's house – not as spartan as it sounds. That
gives more time with Bina and the children. She
talks of her close friend Rita in Calcutta.

'How we loved to talk to each other, Uncle' she said to me. 'When Shaji and Mahdeb were away we were together with our children. Now I have no one. Shaji left the computer and e-mail facility with the team there. So I cannot talk to her on e-mail.'

Happily good friends of mine from Aberdeen have made it possible for us to supply a state-of-the-art computer with e-mail facility. Soon Bina and Rita will be back in contact: small things can be so vital in helping a sense of wellbeing to continue. I learn that many OM folk and relief workers will make contact with this small family. And Bina will soon pick up the language – Indians are often superb linguists.

Ghandhidham is the chosen place for OM's base in the area. The team will grow. Direct evangelism in the villages is not possible. India is very different in this respect from 25 years ago when I first came here. But neighbouring Nepal has proved that the gospel-in-action brings great dividends – witness the incredible growth of the Nepalese church.

OM have been invited to assist three villages in particular. The material help is without strings: it is given to all, whatever their caste or religion. Mother Theresa told me before she died 'to go to the poorest of the poor in India'. This is what Good Shepherd Relief Ministries is all about. OM will arrange for the building of hundreds of houses. The cost to the organisation is £1,100; the villagers will provide the labour. All houses in many villages were destroyed; the loss of life is devastating.

Earthquakes are an 'act of God'. But as I was reminded, basically, they don't kill. The deaths in India were largely through inadequate building and corruption in the building industry. No flexibility was incorporated into the design of the houses and poor materials were used. Earthquakes however can have positive spin-offs. In one village nothing was stolen from the exposed grocery shop. The iniquitous caste system, which is a curse, was broken down. The human tragedy is great however – witness Anadu Bhai saw 31 people die in front of him at the school at Anjar, where a wall fell on the pupils who were marching in a Republic Day celebration.

OM is working with two other groups – the Discipleship Centre based in Delhi and an organisation known as World Relief. They are targeting three villages – Gamaro, Khokra and Tappar, as well as working in Jamnagar – building 33 houses. The houses will have one large bedroom, kitchen, toilet, bathroom and two verandas. They are superior to the accommodation that was destroyed and hopefully will be 'earthquake proof'. The project will last four months with completion before Christmas. OM is thinking of long-term strategy for this area. The tribal people here – the Kholies – are unreached by the gospel. Another advantage of the earthquake is this opening amongst them. These people have not faired well in the caste system of India.

Thursday July 26

I wake around 6.00 a.m. after a good sleep. We take a light breakfast and head off to the relief agencies' office. I meet with others working on this joint project. We have a time of prayer and I am asked to preach. I was reading from Judges earlier in the morning and a verse there provides a springboard into an unscripted address: 'Village life was destroyed in Deborah's day'. I developed the theme – God and the poor, his bias towards the underprivileged and the joy of ministering in his name. I moved forward to Matthew 25 – 'I was sick and you looked after me ...' – and then I move on to one of the Bible's final verses, where we are told in Revelation that our righteous acts are as fine linen on the day of the Lord. He sees all – in Glasgow and Goragphur. We have some prayer.

Nothing however could have prepared me emotionally for the next three hours. We spend some time retracing our route of yesterday. Then Shaji tells the driver to veer away from the main road. After 20 minutes we are definitely in earthquake territory and amongst the Kholies.

Some readers of these journals kindly tell me they are able to 'see' things when I describe them in written form. Any gifting in this area is challenged to breaking point. How does one put into words what is in view? Here are two whole communities wiped out as far as their houses are concerned. In morning devotions I referred to Revelation, the final book in the Bible. It speaks also of the return of Christ and some who, fearing his judgements, call to the rocks to fall on them. That is literally what happened here. I was hardly to know that the spontaneous ministry of the early morning would, two hours later, yield dramatic illustration.

Within three minutes village life was destroyed, the devastation total. A four-storey building collapsed. It had a domino effect on neighbouring houses. A Hindu temple, in the process of being built, is in ruins. Marble-sculptured columns were left as shoots sprouting out at absurd angles from the rubble. A doctor's home fronted by a clinic was totally unrecognisable. Syringes, capsules and the like were strewn all over the deep rubble, evidence of what had

been the nearest equivalent in this area to a hospital.
Yards away is the crushed ambulance jeep meant to
run victims to the hospice, itself a casualty of the
catastrophe. Amazingly, the doctor and his child
were pulled out of the wreckage after some days sub-
merged. It seemed sacrilegious to clamber over the
ruins of what had been people's homes and had also
become their tombs. I imagined the scene thinking of
my own paranoia in the face of intense darkness.
What must it have been like! In this remote place
help could not have come for days – only the bleeding hands of villagers who themselves were suffering
from shock were used in an attempt to achieve the
impossible. Without tools how do you dig them out?
'Good God above where were you in all this? Where
is the mercy? Where is the justice? Were these
people greater sinners than those plying the prostitution racket in Bombay, condemning hundreds of
girls to Aids, taking their virginity?' My 'Christian
agnosticism' spills out. Some things I do not understand. If the Psalmist can ask his questions so can
we. I weep.

Eventually my tears dry – we have to be on our
way. And I think of positive things that emerge
from catastrophe – the sheer goodness of people
who in the face of this disaster have tried and
are trying to alleviate the situation. What about
Bina, forfeiting the security of Calcutta? And
Gideon the OM state leader: he confesses his
peace of mind is disturbed at night by the

mental images that constantly float into his conscious as he reflects on what he encountered when first on the scene. What about the OM lads who are spearheading this village relief programme? Their ill-equipped tent is home – open to all, including the greedy mosquitoes and unclean flies – as they spend time helping the earthquake-shocked villagers build new homes. What about the caste structure in the village that collapsed with the walls of the houses? People in need cling to each other irrespective of breeding and background. Thank God for individuals and trustees of funds who made sums available to OM and me – the sheer honest-to-goodness folk in the West, including some of my students, who gave of their little and hoped that the power behind the multiplication of loaves and fishes is still in some way available today.

Sometimes I think of the Lord's distress over Jerusalem.

India, how often we weep for you – your poverty alongside your opulence, your kindness alongside the corruption. Millions of pounds given at government level for the relief of the poor – yet 90 per cent allegedly lies in government coffers. The day of reckoning shall come when justice will be seen to be done. The stones cry out. The rubble shall yet give way to the power of God. From the severity of his mercies shall arise a new age where righteousness shall flood the earth and goodness shall prevail. Wishful thinking? No, logical deduction from the inspired word. And until then? We go to the poorest of the poor, the most ignorant of the ignorant, with that same word of life. We go armed with our loaves and fishes, with the power of prayer and the knowledge that the God of the Bible is the God of the poor and, though his providence is mysterious with a perplexing darker side, from the 'hidden' God (as Luther put it) will yet emerge his overall fiat. And on that day the universe will witness that righteousness has prevailed.

Friday July 27

I wake around 5.00 a.m. My plane for Hyderabad leaves at 7.50 a.m. and then there will be both the traffic and the animals to negotiate! Shaji has accompanied me for the flight – he was to go by train but I have sufficient cash to help with an airfare. We successfully connect with our driver from the OM base and immediately on arrival at this spacious compound, boasting a huge warehouse, library and auditoria, I go to our board meeting, which has already started. Our new chairman, Revd Johnson, handles affairs firmly as we listen to different reports and make a few decisions. Europeans this time are not allowed to stay at the base, so we resort to a local hotel for a good sleep.

I take what will turn out to be the first of three devotional sessions and speak 40 minutes or so. By now our ranks have swelled to around 150. State leaders and secondary level leaders have gathered from all over India. This will be a day for hearing reports. I think away the decades, two to be precise. Nana Chowk, an area of Bombay floods, comes into my mind – the first headquarters of OM that I knew – with its rats, and noise and incredible loos! From that spartan beginning, an unpretentious acorn has grown this massive oak.

Coming back from my mental wanderings, I pick up on the conference. Reference is being made to a private member's bill being moved in Parliament today to make conversion illegal. The Muslim community, along with the Christians, is contending it. People in Orissa, we are told, are being compelled to return to Hinduism. The Dalits – the untouchable classes – 250 million of them – are threatening to 'convert' to Buddhism as a protest of being so badly treated within Hinduism. Talk is of one million of them coming to Delhi for a mass protest. They have known oppression from the 'Brahminical' ordering of society for centuries – the caste system is obscene. India does not wish it to be discussed by the United Nations – it is an 'internal' matter. But this did not stop them denouncing apartheid in South Africa. The caste system is a more sophisticated and arguably more diabolical manifestation of the same thing – racism.

We hear a number of reports from the Good Shepherd Relief Ministries of OM. This division largely represents OM's social and philanthropic activity, coupled with attempts to promote the gospel. We hear of maltreatment of children numbering tens of thousands in some areas. It is not hype. The *Bombay Times*, which I read on my first internal flight, spoke of the appalling increase in prostitution. Children are bought in Nepal and sell sex in the red light area. The average age of a child prostitute has dropped to 12. Paedophilia would be a more accurate description of the crime.

Bombay has the largest slum in the world; OM has a team working in Dharavi. Move to the opposite side of the city and you will see opulence undreamed of – such contrasts are found in this country. In Sivakasi, Tamil Nadu, 50,000 children work in the fireworks factories, often losing some of their fingers in the process and dying early because of inhaling the chemicals. They are paid around 60 pence a day. OM has opened Lighthouse Primary School. It is hoped they will be allowed to buy some land and increase the intake of children to 1,000. Recently a factory caught fire – one imagines the consequences. There has been no rain for a long time thus water has to be bought for everything.

Tuesday July 31

My flight to Bombay left at 4.00 p.m. and with no problems allowed me to be in this vast, sprawling city by 6.00 p.m. to be met again by Willie who, alas, had to battle through traffic unbelievable to the Westerner – not that we are free of jams, but the roads . . . ! Why not use concrete – the monsoon dislodges all the repairs of tarmac leaving treacherous potholes, more dangerous because they are full of water. I arrive safely, none the less, at Stephen Alfred's home.

Wednesday August 1 – Friday August 3

I had already requested in preparation for this trip that a good part of one day be spent amongst the tribals in the vast areas around Bombay. It is extraordinary that you can be near one of the biggest cities in the world and never know of it! Amongst the tribals is the greatest challenge to Christianity.

Mani is a man I wanted to meet. Stephen spoke so highly of him. Converted from a fairly hideous strain of Hinduism, he has become an outstanding evangelist. He hails from south India and was a devotee of Ayyappa, a deity venerated in Kerala and a particularly ferocious god. Mani used to pass a huge needle through his cheeks, expose his feet to the fire, skewer the skin on the side of his stomach with clips and be in a frenzy for several hours. Added to this would be his annual 40-mile climb in the hills to scale a mountain to offer sacrificial worship. All this in bare feet: it makes the London marathon seem a little more attractive. Mani came to the Lord via Abraham, a local evangelist. Mani's nephew was upset and wanted to meet Abraham to threaten him, deal with him. He thought Abraham would be frightened of him, but he liked Abraham and became a Christian.

We met up with Mani and Abraham in Kinnavlli. He was all that Stephen suggested: a man of medium height; well proportioned with jet-black hair crowning his dark face. In his somewhat humble home he had assembled a number of believers. Three men from the hills had walked fourteen kilometres to meet us. They sat bunched together in a corner looking a little bemused at the proceedings. Joining us was a highly successful Indian businessman and chairman of Bethany Trust, Thomas Matthew. Stephen was alongside me with Alfonso, Stephen's right-hand man, and our driver. The group grew to around two dozen. Food had been carefully prepared – a delicacy was before us, or so I was told. Happily they did not fill my plate as full as the others.

I learned that Abraham, Mani and Mr Thonelu, a brother from an assembly in Thane, spend the whole of Thursday in evangelism. They cover an area for three hours in a morning, then have lunch, followed by three hours of more door-to-door work. Then they have 'dinner', a bath (which has to be Indian style – let him that readeth understand!). They then engage in Bible study from 9.00 p.m. – 1.00 a.m.(!!), only to rise again on Friday at 5.00 a.m. for another three hours.

The village where Abraham lives is called Dolkam. The Edinburgh Medical Missionary Society are donating finances in order to purchase land on which to build a clinic, community hall and a house for the evangelist. Abraham and Hannah and their two children deserve better accommodation than what they have survived in for some years. Witness the tarpaulin strung inside their primitive house under the roof in order to try and keep out some of the unwelcome monsoon. Hannah is the daughter of an evangelist and has a radiance and love for the Lord that befits a person with such a name. Abraham's involvement in this pioneer work, for such it is, devolves from the time he came to the hospital for an operation on his leg. He saw Stephen and Thomas Matthews, one of the trustees, come back from this village and determined to give up his job.

With no training he took on the role of an evangelist and has absorbed so much medical
knowledge that the tribals consider him to be
their doctor. Stephen supplied me with the
information with a mixture of pride and
humour. As soon as Abraham saw Dolkam he
said 'This is where God wants me to be' – and
that was seven years ago.

The work of Bethany Hospital is becoming
multifaceted. The first Aids seminars will be
given this weekend. Stephen is most encouraged by the response of the churches
– particularly the charismatic. Aids is taking
sadistic vengeance amongst the Indians and in
the slums.

'The best thing to do', says the doctor, 'is not
to bring them to the hospital but to create centres where they can be housed and looked after
in the slums.'

He is thinking of groups of three or four.
They will need a lot of care and the slum-
dwellers' help in looking after them. This is
where the seminarians will come in and func-
tion practically. Not all Aids sufferers are to be
blamed. Some contract it through bad blood
and are infected by others – open cuts are
potential entry points for the savage disease.

The hospital is also offering scholarships for poten-
tial doctors. One astonishing story surrounds a
tribal lad from Bihari, one of India's largest, poorest

and racially most divisive states. He lived in a small village; his parents farmed land. (I tap up the story as the monsoon drops gallons of rain.) Until this lad finished schooling he did not know that there was any life outside his village! But in an all-India entrance examination he came 160th. He converted to Christianity and after three years in the faith has read most Christian apologetic books available in the land. He links into what is known as the 'Layman's Evangelical Fellowship', one of the strongest indigenous groups in India: fiercely independent, it eschews Western support. Atul's basic problem was 'Who can take away my sin?' He found no answers in Hinduism. He is now in his fifth and final year at Bombay University and had no finance to complete his course. Thus the help from Bethany Trust.

Friday August 3

I go to the hospital to meet the staff and have a couple of medical checks myself – never did get time in Glasgow! It seems as though I will live a little longer. We leave and head out into the monsoon weather. Stephen and I planned a few hours off. We head to the outskirts of Thane where a few colleagues have bought some land and have erected a block of apartments and sunk a swimming pool. We sink into the pool and relax, fortified later by a delicious Indian meal. This is the first time I have taken a couple of hours off in 12 days. It's good to talk and swim. We return to the hospital and I conduct a short Bible study and have some time with the staff. I have come to love these folk over the years. There is Minnie, a dedicated nurse who battles with failing eyesight, though she is relatively young. Then there is Sister Juliet, who keeps everyone in order – firmly efficient, a good way to describe her. Then there is Grace, who lives up to her name. Tragically bereaved in her early 40s, she has a teenage daughter to look after. Insufficient funds caused her to look for a job. If a 'right-hand man' can be a woman, this is what Grace is to Stephen. He can trust her with the admin-istration department, assessing of payments, in gathering of finances etc. She had wished her daughter to be a doctor and I had offered to sponsor her. Alas, she did not get sufficiently high grades but is being trained in computing. Then there is Alfonso, another Godsend for Stephen. Alfonso is medium build, good looking and has amassed a fund of medical knowledge though has no qualifications. Devoted to Stephen, his input removes many burdens from the doctor – he can concentrate on more serious aspects of his work leaving Alfonso to deal with smaller though vitally important things. Alfonso has a great heart of compassion. He needs it – every alternate day an Aids patient is admitted to this busy place.

Joseph just turned up and started to work. Contract, hours, payment – never came into it. Self-appointed, he saw the site, decided there was something for him to do – and he does it. Groundsman and caretaker, he has turned the land around the hospital into a garden. It is hard to contrast this institution with others. It is clean and attractive. The stonework is emulsioned every year. The marble glistens, there are forms for people to sit on to benefit from the garden. Joseph seems to be there when something needs to be done. Now he is able to fetch his wife, and a former nurses' home (funded by my old church) will be made available for them – the first time they have lived under the same roof consistently for seven years.

I have a concern for the Alfreds. The flat they live in does not adequately supply their needs. Constantly travelling in and out of the hospital are visitors and supporters, doctors and representatives of funding agencies. Stephen and his never-complaining wife, Claire, put them up. Their delightful lads surrender their beds. But I think on to when these lads will be students, and their need of room. A small block of houses arranged in a semicircle form a compound at the back of the huge block of flats where Stephen lives. When I was here six months ago, I walked round the block and thought it would be good for Stephen to have a larger house with an annexe for guests. A man came out to speak to me and I talked about the dwellings. Incredibly he has put his house on the market. Stephen has the first offer. A deposit has been paid. The deal is sealed. We now need to raise £25,000 by the end of August – another faith challenge! The sense and logic behind the purchase are unassailable.

Stephen wants me to spend the evening with the hospital trustees, though one, a lady doctor, is unable to be present. With KV Simon (a Brethren Assemblies leader in the Bombay area) and Thomas Matthew we review the hospital's growth and development over seven years. There are two boards – one in the UK and the other here in India. We contrast what was intended, the initial vision, with what has developed, the realised vision. The latter transcends the former, leaving us astounded at providence. The intensive care unit, three floors fully operational with the fourth ready to take in street children whose circumstances sometimes are too terrible to relate, are witness to the reality of the Spirit's leading. The man who walks on water at the request of the Lord is not left looking foolish – though the strains of getting out of the boat, leaving the comfort zone and taking risks are considerable.

Saturday August 4

I am sitting in the airport lounge in Bombay. I arrived here at 4.00 a.m. for a flight that still has two hours to departure. How much time I have spent in airport lounges during the last 20 years or so! This one has improved considerably. KLM's efficiency meant a speedy check-in with no problem with my baggage weight (which must be twice the allowance). Printing in India is cheap and I had 1,000 booklets printed for ICC, most of which I have been hauling around.

I reflect on the itinerary. To fail to achieve some goals would render the visit inappropriate in terms of cost, expenditure of nervous energy. If you don't think there is any loss of the latter you should try Bombay/Thane roads: even when the traffic is sparse at three in the morning, hazards are prolific. Witness the lorry with no lights and an overhanging load, barely discernible at 20 feet. Potholes and proliferate speed bumps, always unmarked: just an extra, needless hazard.

In the early morning as I start my journey back to the West I think of the 13-year-old drug addict, who is also an alcoholic, brought in by the Oasis team just 2 days ago. A wizened old man – that is how he looked – and yet hardly into his teens, one of the tens of thousands of jetsam and flotsam that bob around in Bombay, Calcutta and all the cities and towns. This fellow required eight bottles of blood – these sell at around

1,600 rupees a bottle (£30), a massive sum in India. He was found on the railway station having defecated and urinated for two days in his own mess, an old man for whom the years of youth passed by and never stopped. His haemoglobin count was down to 2.2 as opposed to the normal 14. Eight out of ten pavement boys so rescued do not return to the streets. I think of the plans now being worked on for three years for a halfway house in Calcutta – such is needed in Bombay. The Oasis team is to be congratulated on their dedication to sharing the love of Jesus in such a tangible way. And so are OM and Stephen and a host of others 'of whom the world is not worthy' – men and women who in serving the Lord expend themselves. And in the expenditure they preach a sermon, the notes of which are recorded in heaven. The life of obedience is registered on celestial computers. The First Missionary declared that his gospel is to circumnavigate the world. But it will not be in word only or in Spirit only. To the word and the Spirit will be added acts of mercy that heighten the credibility of the holistic gospel of Christ. 'Go not just to the poor, but the poorest of the poor...' Mother Theresa's words ring in my ears and though it was seven years ago since I was with her, it seems only like yesterday.

Many thanks to all who remembered this venture in prayer. And to those who gave money and medical equipment.

Tony Sargent is Principal of International Christian College, Glasgow.

ZONDERVAN

Philip Yancey is one of the world's best-selling Christian author. His 16 books include *Where Is God When It Hurts?*, *Disappointment With God*, *The Jesus I Never Knew* and *What's so Amazing About Grace?* He writes articles and a monthly column for *Christianity Today* magazine which he serves as Editor At Large. He also serves as co-chair of the editorial board for *Books and Culture*, a recent publication of *Christianity Today*.

Living In Faith

by Philip Yancey

To live in the past and future is easy.
To live in the present is like threading a needle.
Walker Percy

My pastor in Chicago, Bill Leslie, said he often felt like an old hand-operated water pump, the kind still found in some camp-grounds. Everyone who came to him for help would pump vigorously a few times, and each time he felt something drain out of him. Ultimately he reached a place of spiritual emptiness, with nothing more to give. He felt dry, desiccated.

In the midst of this period, Bill went on a week-long retreat and bared his soul to his assigned spiritual director, a nun. He expected her to offer soothing words about what a sacrificial, unselfish person he was, or perhaps recommend a sabbatical. Instead she said, 'Bill, there's only one thing to do if your reservoir runs dry. You've got to go deeper.' He returned from that retreat convinced that his faith depended less on his outer journey of life and ministry than on his inner journey toward spiritual depth.

In the foothills of the Rocky Mountains where I live, well-diggers drilled down 640 feet before striking water for our house. Even then the water only trickled until they used a technique called 'fracking', short for hydro-fracturing. Pumping water down the well shaft at very high pressure, technicians shattered the granite into gravel and opened new seams for water flow. As I watched, pressures that to me seemed likely to destroy the well actually tapped new sources of water. I'm sure Bill Leslie would appreciate the analogy: extreme pressures, seemingly destructive, forced him to seek new sources of strength – the very reason he had pursued spiritual direction in the first place.

In a similar metaphor, the prophet Jeremiah writes of a bush that sets its roots in parched desert soil. In times of rainfall and prosperity the plant flourishes, but during drought its shallow roots shrivel and die. Jeremiah draws a contrast to the one who lives in faith:

> . . . blessed is the man who trusts in the Lord,
>   whose confidence is in him.
> He will be like a tree planted by the water
>   that sends out its roots by the stream.
> It does not fear when heat comes;
>   its leaves are always green.

It has no worries in a year of drought
    and never fails to bear fruit.

The Bible makes no rosy promises about living
only in springtime. Instead, it points toward faith
that helps us prepare for arid seasons. Harsh
winters will come, followed by scorching summers. Yet if the roots of faith go deep enough,
tapping into Living Water, we can survive the
drought times and flourish in times of plenty.

* * *

According to Stanley Hauerwas, the life of faith
consists of patience and hope. When something
comes along to test our relationship with God,
we rely on those two virtues: patience formed
by a long memory; and hope that our faithfulness will prove worth the risk. Jews and
Christians have always emphasised these
virtues, Hauerwas notes, for we believe that a
God who is both good and faithful controls the
universe; patience and hope keep faith alive
during times that cast doubt on that belief.

I would paraphrase Hauerwas by saying the
life of faith consists of living in the past and in
the future. I live in the past in order to ground
myself in what God has already done, as a way
of gaining confidence in what he might do
again. Relating to an invisible God involves certain handicaps: with no sensory evidence in the
present, we must look backward to remind

ourselves of who it is we are relating to. Every time God introduced himself as 'the God of Abraham, Isaac, and Jacob', he reminded his chosen people of his history with them – a history that for all three forebears included seasons of testing and doubt.

I too learn about faith by looking back at Abraham, Isaac and Jacob, for God proceeded in a most puzzling manner with all three. After God had promised to bring about a people as numerous as the stars in the sky, what followed more resembled a case study in family infertility. Abraham and Sarah entered their 90s before they saw their first child; that son (appropriately named Isaac, or 'laughter') married a barren woman; the grandson, Jacob, had to wait 14 years for the wife of his dreams, only to discover her barren as well. This tortuous path toward populating a great nation shows that God operates on a different timetable than impatient human beings expect. From Abraham, Isaac and Jacob – and also Joseph, Moses, David and a host of others – I learn that God moves in ways I would neither predict nor desire. Yet each of those Old Testament characters lived and died in faith, vowing to the end that God had indeed kept his promises.

All through the Psalms, David and the other poets peer over their shoulders to former times when God appeared powerless yet somehow triumphed, when trust seemed foolhardy yet proved prudent. Psalms that review the history of God's deliverance often betray the writer's misgivings over whether God will intervene so spectacularly again. Strong memories soothe a restless present, as any number of psalms can attest.

New Testament letters advise the same: study the Scriptures diligently, as necessary road maps for contests of faith. Beyond the Bible, the testimony of the entire church bears witness of God's faithfulness. Where would my own faith be, I wonder, without Augustine, Donne, Dostoevsky, Jürgen Moltmann, Thomas Merton, C.S. Lewis? Many times I have leaned on their words as an exhausted traveller might lean against a roadside monument.

'I find that I crave light as a thirsting man craves water,' wrote Commander Richard Byrd during a six-month sojourn in a metal hut at the South Pole. In the Antarctic winter, the sun made no appearance for four of those months. 'A funereal gloom hangs in the twilight sky. This is the period between life and death. This is the way the world will look to the last man when it dies.' Three weeks before the sun was due to return, he wrote in his journal about the sun's reappearance, 'I tried to imagine what it would be like, but the conception was too vast for me to grasp.' How strange those words must have seemed when Byrd later edited that journal for publication, living out his days in a latitude that saw the sun's rays every day.

Although I do not keep a formal journal, my writings accomplish something similar. I pick up an article I wrote 25 years ago and marvel at the passion I felt over an issue I have hardly thought about since. Such anger, doubt, barely controlled cynicism! I find cries of lament pencilled long ago in the margins of my Bible and give thanks that I made it through that particular valley. When exuberant, I look at my past writings and am shocked at the sloughs of despond I wallowed in; when depressed, I am shocked at the bright faith I used to have. Mainly, from the past I gain perspective that what I feel and believe right now I will not always feel and believe – which drives me to sink roots deeper, into layers of subsoil unaffected by El Niño or other vagaries of climate.

Remembering my relationship with God takes effort and intentionality. I cannot pull out a home video and watch our history and growth together; there are no photo albums of living in faith. I must consciously work at reviewing both the progress of the ache and the progress of the healing.

Reflecting on his own life, the apostle Paul wrote, 'Here is a trustworthy saying that deserves full acceptance: Christ Jesus came into the world to save sinners – of whom I am the worst. But for that very reason I was shown mercy so that in me, the worst of sinners, Christ Jesus might display his unlimited patience.' I imagine many people would dispute Paul for that title 'worst of sinners'. Paul looks back just long enough to remember his former state and to stake his claim, then turns ahead to the future: 'Now to the King eternal, immortal, invisible, the only God, be honour and glory for ever and ever. Amen.'

The creek by my house freezes over every winter. If I bend down close, though, I can hear it flowing beneath the ice, the sound muffled but unmistakable. Never does it stop. Under the frigid layers of winter lies proof of an inevitable summer.

* * *

Of patience and hope, past and future, the life of faith consists. Martin Marty, who rated half the psalms as 'wintry' in tone, also noted that 149 of the 150 eventually get around to hope.

Jürgen Moltmann, one of the premier theologians of our time, recounts in the slim book *Experiences of God* his personal journey toward hope. Drafted as a teenager in World War II, he was sent to the German front, where the British soon captured him. The next three years he spent in detention, shuttled from prison camp to prison camp in Belgium, Scotland and

England. Meanwhile Hitler's empire collapsed, exposing the moral rot at the centre of the Third Reich, and all around him Moltmann saw how other Germans 'collapsed inwardly, how they gave up all hope, sickening for the lack of it, some of them dying. The same thing almost happened to me. What kept me from it was a rebirth to new life . . . '

Apart from the cultural trappings of Christmas and other holidays, Moltmann had no Christian background. He had brought just two books with him into battle: Goethe's poems and the complete works of Nietzsche, in editions that Hitler had distributed to his troops. Neither nourished hope, to put it mildly. But a chaplain gave him a New Testament, which included the Psalms in an appendix.

'If I make my bed in hell, behold thou art there,' Moltmann the prisoner read. Could God be present in that dark night? 'I was dumb with silence, I held my peace, even from good; and my sorrow was stirred . . . I am a stranger with thee, and a sojourner, as all my fathers were.' As he read, Moltmann found words that perfectly captured his own feelings of desolation. He became convinced that God 'was present even behind the barbed wire – no, most of all behind the barbed wire'.

As Moltmann kept reading, he also found something new in the Psalms: hope. Walking the perimeter of the barbed wire at night for exercise, he would circle a small hill in the centre of the camp, on which stood a hut that served as a chapel. For him the hut became a symbol of God's presence radiating in the midst of suffering, and out of that symbol grew hope.

Upon release, Moltmann abandoned his plan to study quantum physics and turned instead to theology, founding a movement called 'a theology of hope'. We on earth exist, he concluded, in a state of contradiction between the cross and the resurrection. Surrounded by decay, we none the less hope for perfection, for a restoration of the cosmos. We have no proof that it can ever be attained, only a sign in history, the 'foreglow' of the raising of Christ from the dead. Yet if we can sustain faith in that glorious future, it can transform the present – just as Moltmann's own hope of eventual release from prison camp transformed his daily experience there.

A future faith can alter the present, at the very least by allowing us to suspend judgement of God. A person without future faith logically assumes that the suffering and chaos on this planet reflect something of God; therefore, God is neither all-good nor all-powerful. Future faith allows me to believe that God is not satisfied with this world either and plans to restore the universe to its original design. Just as Moltmann came to believe in the possibility of life outside a prison camp someday, I can believe in a future time when God will reign with perfect justice.

'Away distrust: My God hath promised, he is just,' wrote George Herbert. I need that reminder daily. With future faith, I can trust in that as-yet-unverified justice despite all the apparent contradictions on this groaning planet.

* * *

In his autobiography, *A Long Walk to Freedom*, Nelson Mandela recalls the scene when he first laid eyes on his granddaughter. At the time, he was working at hard labour on Robben Island in almost unbearable conditions, cutting lime in a quarry under a sun so bright it nearly blinded him. Only one thing kept the prisoners from despair, he writes: they sang together as they worked. The songs reminded them of family and home and tribe and the world outside they might otherwise forget.

During the 14th year of his imprisonment, Mandela gained permission for a visit from his daughter (he was generally forbidden visitors). She ran across the room and embraced him. Mandela had not held his daughter since she was a young girl, and it was both poignant and dizzying to hug this fully-grown woman, his child. Then she handed over her own newborn baby, Nelson's granddaughter, into his callused, leathery hands. 'To hold a newborn baby, so vulnerable and soft in my rough hands, hands that for too long had held only picks and shovels, was a profound joy. I don't think a man was ever happier to hold a baby than I was that day.'

Mandela's tribal culture had a tradition of letting the grandfather choose a new baby's name, and Nelson toyed with various names as he held that tiny, helpless baby. He settled on Zaziwe, which means Hope. 'The name had special meaning for me, for during all my years in prison hope never left me – and now it never would. I was convinced that this child would be a part of a new generation of South Africans for whom apartheid would be a distant memory – that was my dream.'

As it turned out, Mandela had served barely half his sentence and would not gain freedom for 13 more years. The vision of hope, however, of Zaziwe, sustained him. Despite little present evidence at the time, he believed that the reality of apartheid in South Africa would someday crumble. The time would come, whether in his lifetime or his granddaughter's, when a new kind of justice would descend. Future faith determined his present.

Even for those who, unlike Mandela, do not live to see hope realised in this life, future faith holds out hope in resurrection. Dallas Willard knew a woman who refused to talk about life beyond death because, she said, she did not want her children to be disappointed if it turned out no afterlife existed. As Willard points out, if no afterlife exists, no one will have any consciousness with which to feel disappointment! On the other hand, if there is an afterlife, shouldn't we prepare for it?

When I lived in Chicago, we watched the steady physical deterioration in a church member named Sabrina. Young, slender, beautiful, stylish, Sabrina caught the eye of every man and the envy of every woman until an inoperable brain tumour began its cruel work on her. Every month our church had a time of prayer for healing, and Sabrina and her husband went forward each month. Soon she was wearing colourful scarves to hide the effects of the chemotherapy. All too quickly, she began walking with a limp, in need of assistance just to make it down the aisle. Then she lost the use of all her limbs and attended church in a wheelchair. Then she went blind and was confined to bed. Toward the end, she could not speak and communicated by blinking her eyes at her husband's promptings.

Those of us who knew Sabrina cried out to God on her behalf. The pastors anointed her with oil. We wished and prayed for a miracle. We felt helpless and angry as our prayers went unanswered and we watched the inexorable progress of the disease.

At Sabrina's funeral, held in the same church, about half of those in attendance came from the congregation and half from her workplace. Her colleagues at work stared at the hymn books and the liturgy on the programme as if they were written in a foreign language. All of us, regardless of faith background or beliefs, shared the sense of grief and outrage at what had happened to Sabrina. Yet her husband, her pastors, and her fellow-parishioners also shared something incomprehensible to the others attending: hope that Sabrina's life had not truly ended, hope that we would one day see her again.

'Lord, to whom shall we go?' asked Simon Peter in a moment of confusion. I feel his words deeply at every funeral I attend. Without resurrection faith, belief in a future beyond what we now know, death has the last word and proclaims its mocking victory. A 'foreglow' of resurrection surely does not dispel the shadows, but it does bathe them in the new light of hope.

* * *

Leo Tolstoy, who did not disdain adding a moral lesson to his stories, ended his short story 'Three Questions' this way: 'Remember then: there is only one time that is important – Now! It is the most important time because it is the only time when we have any power.'

A record of God's faithfulness in the past combines with hope in a better future for one end: to equip us for the present. As Tolstoy said, we have control over no other time. The past is unchangeable, the future unpredictable. I can only live the life directly before me. Faithful Christians pray, 'Thy will be done, on earth as it is in heaven', and then proceed to enact God's will – love, justice, peace, mercy, forgiveness – in the present, on earth.

I have learned the importance of the present, by analogy, in the writing process. If I focus on previous books and articles I have written, fretting over my failures and relishing my successes, or if I concentrate on the future, worrying about deadlines and carrying the whole book in my mind, I will undergo paralysis in the present. I must devote myself to the word and sentence before me, to the present moment.

My friends in recovery groups live by the indispensable slogan 'One day at a time'. The historian of Alcoholics Anonymous titled his work *Not-God* because, he said, the most important hurdle an addicted person must surmount is to acknowledge deep in the soul that he or she is not God. No mastery of manipulation and control, at which alcoholics excel, can overcome the root problem; rather, the alcoholic must recognise his or her own helplessness and fall back in the arms of the Higher Power. 'First of all we had to quit playing God,' concluded the founders of AA. Next, we must in faith allow God himself to 'play God' in our lives, which involves daily, even moment-by-moment surrender.

If I reflect on my entire spiritual pilgrimage at once, I usually end up nostalgic for those times when God seemed so much closer. Faith, I have found, is not something I settle into, a skill I learn to master. It comes as a gift from God, and I need to pray for it every day, as I pray for daily bread. A friend of mine, paralysed in an accident, traces her turning point in faith to this very principle. She could not face a life of total paralysis; she could, however, face one day at a time, with God's help. The Bible contains 365 commands to 'fear not' – the most reiterated command in the Bible – as if to remind us daily that we will face difficulties that might naturally provoke fear.

'There is no fear in love', writes the apostle John, 'but perfect love drives out fear ...' He goes on to point to the source of that perfect love: 'We love because he first loved us.' In other words, the cure to fear is not a change in circumstances, rather a deep grounding in the love of God. I ask God to reveal his love to me directly, or through my relationships with those who also know him – a prayer I think God takes great delight in answering. When I get depressed about my present failures, I ask God to remind me of my true identity: one who will be made perfect and has already been forgiven.

'You've got to go deeper,' said the nun to my burned-out pastor. Sink the well into a water table that never runs dry.

Thomas Merton conceded that everything in modern city life conspires against such a surrender. We worry about money, about what we need to have and to know, about whom to compete with, and what is slipping out of our control. Ultimately this agitation, which Merton termed a 'neurosis', drove him into a monastery, where at last he found a place for quietness and meditation. In fact, Merton's autobiography recounts the day he decided to enter the monastery rather than the army. In either course he would find happiness, he believed, if that were the course God wanted for him. 'There is only one happiness: to please Him. Only one sorrow, to be displeasing to Him . . .'

Merton found the secret to true freedom: If we live to please God alone, we set ourselves free from the cares and worries that press in on us. So many of my own cares trace back to concern over other people: whether I measure up to their expectations, whether they find me desirable. Living for God alone involves a radical reorientation, a stripping away of anything that might lure me from the primary goal of pleasing God. Living in faith involves me pleasing God, far more than God pleasing me.

I know a hand surgeon who specialises in reattaching fingers that have been partially or completely severed in accidents. When he enters the operating room, he knows he will be squinting into a microscope for six to eight hours, sorting out and stitching together the snarl of nerves, tendons, and blood vessels finer than human hairs. A single mistake, and the patient may permanently lose movement or sensation. He cannot take a coffee break or even a bathroom break. Once my friend got an emergency call at three o'clock in the morning and could hardly face the prospect of beginning such an arduous procedure. In order to add incentive and focus, he decided to dedicate the surgery to his father who had recently died. For the next few hours, he imagined his father standing beside him, his hand on his shoulder, offering encouragement.

The technique worked so well that he began dedicating his surgeries to people he knew. He would call them, often awakening them, and say, 'I have a very demanding procedure ahead of me, and I'd like to dedicate the surgery to you. If I think about you while I'm performing it, that will help me get through.' And then it dawned on him: should not he offer his life to God in the same way? The details of what he did each day – answering phone calls, hiring staff, reading medical journals, meeting with patients, scheduling surgeries – changed little, yet somehow the awareness of living for God gradually coloured each of those mundane tasks. He found himself treating nurses with more care and respect, spending more time with patients, worrying less about finances.

* * *

I have visited Calcutta, India, a place of poverty, death, and irremediable human problems. There, the nuns trained by Mother Teresa serve the poorest, most miserable people on the planet: half-dead bodies picked up from the streets of Calcutta. The world stands in awe at the sisters' dedication and the results of their ministry, but something about these nuns impresses me even more: their serenity. If I tackled such a daunting project, I would likely be scurrying about, faxing press releases to donors, begging for more resources, gulping tranquilisers, grasping at ways to cope with my mounting desperation. Not these nuns.

Their serenity traces back to what takes place before their day's work begins. At four o'clock in the morning, long before the sun, the sisters rise, awakened by a bell and the call, 'Let us bless the Lord.' 'Thanks be to God,' they reply. Dressed in spotless white saris, they file into the chapel, where they sit on the floor, Indian-style, and pray and sing together. On the wall of the plain chapel hangs a crucifix with the words 'I thirst'. Before meeting their first 'client', they immerse themselves in worship and in the love of God.

I sense no panic in the sisters who run the
Home for the Dying and Destitute in Calcutta. I
see concern and compassion, yes, but no obses-
sion over what did not get done. In fact, early
on in their work Mother Teresa instituted a rule
that her sisters take Thursdays off for prayer
and rest. 'The work will always be here but if
we do not rest and pray, we will not have the
presence to do our work,' she explained. These
sisters are not working to complete a caseload
sheet for a social service agency. They are working for God. They begin their day with him;
they end their day with him, back in the chapel
for night prayers; and everything in between
they present as an offering to God. God alone
determines their worth and measures their success.

When his life's work was threatened, St
Ignatius of Loyola was asked what he would do
if Pope Paul IV dissolved the Society of Jesus, to
which he had devoted his energy and gifts. He
replied, 'I would pray for fifteen minutes, then
I would not think of it again.'

I cannot pretend to anything like the magis-
terial attitude of Ignatius or Mother Teresa's
nuns. I admire, even revere them, and pray
that some day I will attain something like the
holy simplicity they embody. For now, all I can
muster is a daily (and erratic at that) process of
'centring' my life on God. I want my life to be

integrated in the one true reality of a God who knows everything about me and desires for me only the good. I want to view all the distractions of my day from the perspective of eternity. I want to abandon myself to a God who can elevate me beyond the tyranny of myself. I will never be free from evil, or from distractions, but I pray that I can be freed from the anxiety and unrest that crowd in with them.

In the morning I ask for the grace to live for God alone, and yet when the phone rings with a message that strokes my ego, or when I open a letter from an irate reader, I find myself slipping back – no, tumbling back – to a self-consciousness in which other people, or circumstances, determine my worth and my serenity. I sense my need for transformation and keep going only because that sense is the one sure basis for potential change.

'The motions of Grace; the hardness of heart; external circumstances', Pascal jotted down in one of his cryptic notes. These three things encompass our lives. External circumstances press in: family strife, job pressures, financial worries, global concerns. The motions of grace, God's gifts within, seek to ground us in a deeper reality. Hardness of heart? Of the three, this alone falls somewhat under my control. All I can do is pray daily for God to 'batter my heart', in John Donne's phrase, or better yet, to melt it with his love.

Transformation comes, in the end, not from an act of will, but an act of grace. We can only ask for it and keep asking.

> **There is a Moment in each Day that Satan cannot find.**
> *William Blake*

This chapter is taken from Philip Yancey, *Reaching For The Invisible God*, published by Zondervan, 2000.

The Dalits of India
A cry for freedom

The Dalits of India have been the oppressed majority for more than three thousand years due to the Hindu caste system. These people have experienced an awakening and are now demanding equal human rights and dignity. They believe that rejecting the Hindu caste system and getting an English education are the keys to finding freedom. On November 4, 2001, the Dalit community gathered in New Delhi and on that day, Indian Christians stood in solidarity with the Dalits in their quest for freedom.

In response to an invitation, Christian leaders from all parts of India have decided to start 1000 Dalit Education Centres. The centres will be placed in strategic locations as requested by local Dalit leadership. Each Centre will cater to the primary educational needs of 300-500 children

and built on high academic standards based on the Christian world view about God, human dignity, human salvation and social equality. Each DEC will have a team of competent nationals of at least five school teachers and ten Bible teachers and pioneer workers.

OM India is looking for international partners to join the work of reaching out with God's love to the oppressed of India through Dalit Education Centres. There are several ways in which you, your fellowship or your foundation can get involved. Some potential partnership agreements include:

* Sponsoring the construction of a Dalit Education Centre.
* Sponsoring the annual operational expenses of a Dalit Education Centre.
* Sponsoring a class of students.
* Sponsoring literature needs.

To keep in touch, or to be informed about the Dalit Education Centre Project, please write to the following address:

Rosemary Morris
  India Ministries Co-ordinator
    PO Box 660
      Forest Hill
        London
          SE23 3ST

Operation Mobilisation India

one person
can call for change…

one million people
can become
a movement for change

to be part of
a movement for change
call 08451 207 277
or visit www.eauk.org

evangelical alliance
uniting to change society

Make it a success.

Make it happen.

A big hello from Central Asia.
At the moment some of our
multinational team are very
busy ministering to Afghan
refugees. I'm continuing to visit
my friend Yilduz who became
a Christian three months ago.
Please keep praying for
more workers and increasing
language skills for our team.
Thank you for your ongoing
support and partnership.

Katie.

Greetings!

Join Bible a Month Club and discover an inspiring way to pray, a regular way to give. Together we can provide God's Word in ways that speak to and touch hearts and minds worldwide.

bible society making the bible heard

To find out more about Bible a Month Club, contact Bible Society, Stonehill Green, Westlea, SWINDON, SN5 7DG, telephone 01793 418100 or visit www.biblesociety.org.uk/bamc Charity Registration No. 232759

OPERATION WORLD

Patrick Johnstone & Jason Mandryk

ISBN 1-85078-357-8

This is the definitive prayer guide to the nations, peoples and cities of the world. Completely updated and revised for the first time in eight years, Operation World provides key background information for every country. Major prayer challenges are gathered direct from hundreds of on-site Christian workers across all denominations. Answers to prayer are carefully logged, complete with all-new maps, cross-references, addresses and indexes. Operation World is the most comprehensive, up-to-date, and wide-ranging compilation of prayer information ever produced.

Authentic
LIFESTYLE

STREET GIRLS

Matt Roper

ISBN 1-85078-403-5

This is the story of the Meninadança Project – a charity established to reach out to the street-girls of Belo Horizonte, to offer them a place of security and safety, rehabilitation and re-integration into society. Matt Roper is a vision-ary with a moving story to tell. If you have ever thought, prayed or merely wished for a Christian response to child abuse you should read what Matt has to say and listen to what God has to say to you.

Authentic
LIFESTYLE

SAMARITAN'S PURSE

Operation Christmas Child sends a message of hope to children in desperate situations around the world through gift-filled shoeboxes and Christian literature. This programme provides an opportunity for individuals of all ages to be involved in a simple, hands-on missions project that reaches out to suffering children while focusing on the true meaning of Christmas – Jesus Christ, God's greatest gift. In 2001, Samaritan's Purse collected over 5 million shoeboxes worldwide and distributed them to children in about 95 countries.

First published in 2001 by Paternoster Lifestyle

07 06 05 04 03 02 01   7 6 5 4 3 2 1

Paternoster Lifestyle is an imprint of Authentic Media
PO Box 300, Carlisle, Cumbria, CA3 0QS, UK
and PO Box 1047, Waynesboro, GA 30830-2047, USA
www.paternoster-publishing.com

Operation Christmas Child is a registered trademark of
Samaritan's Purse, a charitable non-profit organisation,
PO Box 3000, Boone, North Carolina 28607,
United States of America

British Library Cataloguing-in-Publication Data

A catalogue record for this book is available from the
British Library

ISBN 1-85078-366-7

Love In A Box

by Emma Carswell

It was December 1990 and a long way from the Christmas rush of Wrexham that the team had left a few days earlier: the contrast could not have been starker. It had only been a few weeks since the first bleak pictures of the children of Romania had been seen in the West. As the shops began to make space for Christmas decorations and brightly coloured lights were strung across the high streets, television screens were presenting a much bleaker prospect for these children. Images of the oppressive orphanages of the Ceausescu regime left very few Britons unmoved by the cruelty and injustice.

Yet, while most of us felt powerless to help, one man in the Welsh border town of Wrexham wasn't prepared to sit and watch their plight from the comfort of his home. Dave Cooke was always one to befriend the downtrodden and to speak up for those who cannot or dare not. He felt the urge to go to Romania himself, to give what he had to those who had nothing.

From the outset of their marriage, Dave and Gill Cooke had made a habit of reading the Bible and praying together. As committed Christians, their relationship with God was right at the centre of their lives, and they regularly asked him for direction. Dave couldn't get the television images out of his head, and began to wonder if this was God prompting him to do something new for him.

A meal with friends John and Carol Roberts had been in the diary for some time, but the timing was perfect. As they ate, the conversation naturally turned to the pictures of the little Romanian kids who had nothing and who were being cruelly treated. Knowing Dave to be impulsive, it was little surprise to everyone when he turned to John and asked, 'Do you fancy driving a truck full of supplies to Romania with me?'

Some months earlier Dave had heard a man speak about his work taking aid into Poland and had thought at the time that this was something he could do. The overwhelming situation in Romania presented him with an opportunity that he could turn into a reality. The adventure had begun.

First thing next morning Dave proposed the idea to his brother Paul and Dai Hughes, a friend with whom he played football. Both agreed to be part of a basic committee that would decide where to go from there. Not appreciating the power of the media, Dave had no idea at this stage that Dai's employers, local radio station Marcher Sound, would take this from being one man's personal vision to a campaign that would capture the heart of the town of Wrexham and beyond.

Looking back, Dave is quick to acknowledge he couldn't have done it on his own: 'Right from the beginning God provided top professionals – God-fearing people who rallied around us and made things happen.' Godfrey Williams was one of these provisions. As Managing Director of Marcher Sound, he immediately caught the vision, jumping at an opportunity to respond to the massive problems in Romania. Between the wholehearted support of the radio station and the local newspaper, the *Wrexham Mail*, they found themselves in the heart of a highly effective PR machine. From day one, things began to happen, and the funds and supplies started pouring in.

Marcher Sound's on-air launch of its Christmas charity project could not have gone better. Presenters described how Romanians had been brutalised by the ruthless dictator Nicolae Ceausescu. They explained how it had been government policy to force women to bear at least four children, regardless of whether they had any means of bringing them up.

This was Operation Christmas Child's first public request for help. Once off air, everyone in the studio waited anxiously for a reaction from the listeners. 'Suddenly all the office phones lit up like Christmas trees,' Dai Hughes recalled. People rang from all over the area – medical staff from Wrexham, Runcorn, Preston and Manchester, physiotherapists from Liverpool, housewives from Chester and Shrewsbury – all offering their help and services. It had provoked an emotional response, and many of the callers were in tears.

Marcher's phone system quickly became jammed and it stayed that way. The public response was snowballing before their eyes. Marcher kept pounding out the story, with Dave joining them on air to explain the goals of Operation Christmas Child. He announced a list of the goods desperately needed in Romania and what would be required to get them there, asking people for 'sacrificial giving'.

A moving account of the Romanians' plight by *Wrexham Mail*'s Chief Reporter Cath Steward widened the impact of the story still further. Within hours, the Marcher studios were swamped with nappies, children's shoes, toys, soap, saucepans, food parcels, bandages, blankets – the list was endless!

What had started as a snowball was quickly turning into an avalanche! Operation

Christmas Child desperately needed help as the idea conceived in Dave's front room was now a campaign that was dominating the region. Marcher decided to set up a reception area in its main office where the public could deliver all their gifts.

Volunteers were quick to offer their help. Wives Jayne Cooke, Carol Roberts and Margaret Peet stepped in to perform innumerable miracles of organisation to restore order out of the chaos in Marcher's foyer.

The involvement of Steve Edmunds, a man with vast experience in dealing with hospitals and drug companies, proved to be a huge asset. Launching a personal mission to gather enough equipment to satisfy all the hospitals in Romania, he began by knocking on doors at his own medical supplies company and Wrexham Maelor Hospital. The response from both was phenomenal, so from there he set off to northern England looking for further help.

Ton after ton of medical equipment started arriving in Wrexham, from defibrillators to portable X-ray machines and from wheelchairs to incubators – even vans full of bandages, dressings, mattresses and crutches. Before long over £500,000 worth of medical equipment was waiting to be delivered to Romania. The original plan to take two trucks was looking a little small scale; to carry all the aid they were now looking at ten lorries.

Operation Christmas Child was outgrowing the foyer at Marcher Sound and there was a desperate need for a warehouse. Dave picked up the phone, dialled the Welsh Development Agency and asked if they could help out by providing a warehouse. In fact, he wasn't just asking for any warehouse: 'We need 25,000 square feet – and I could really do with the one next door to where I work!' The WDA came back with a firm yes, so Operation Christmas Child found themselves with the warehouse of their choice, enabling Dave to manage distributions and deliveries easily.

Dave and Paul Cooke's sister, Jan, who also lived in the Wrexham area, had the brilliant idea of asking every child to wrap a shoebox in Christmas paper and fill it with things another child would enjoy – like a real stocking in a box. The idea was that each shoebox would be sealed with a message of love in the form of a Christmas card or a letter.

Immediately thousands of shoeboxes started to pour in. The idea was simple, personal and fun – and children jumped at it. Such was the response that a van was put to full-time use, visiting schools on a daily basis to collect the thousands of shoeboxes.

On the day of the send off, the *Daily Star* awarded the people of Wrexham its coveted 'Golden Star Award'. Presented in honour of the town's achievement of raising a staggering

£600,000 in cash and aid in just seven weeks to help the suffering Romanian orphans, the *Daily Star* summed up the effort in a simple message – 'Well done wonderful Wrexham'.

On Thursday December 13 1990 Wrexham did itself proud as it turned out in full force to give its mission of mercy to Romania a moving send off. While the team tucked into a full cooked breakfast with the Lord Mayor, over 5,000 people gathered outside the Guildhall.

Despite the bitterly cold December weather, flags were waving, and everyone was cheering and singing along to the music provided by Marcher Sound. Live bands, DJs and a massive carnival were all part of the event. Emotions were highly charged and people were crying everywhere. These men were going into the unknown, and no one was quite sure what they would find.

Dave Cooke's original idea had been to take a couple of trucks over to Eastern Europe. Eventually seven lorries, decorated with tinsel, balloons and messages from the children of Wrexham, revved up their engines and slowly moved through the crowds. Looking out on the sea of faces through their tear-filled eyes, the team of 18 drivers and a film crew could hardly have had a more rousing send off.

On each street corner crowds were queuing to wave them off. No one wanted to miss out on the mission that had brought the whole community together. 'All the drivers agreed that the atmosphere at the send off was amazing,' recalled journalist Paul Wilcox. 'To see all those young people crying, it was almost as though they were experiencing some of the things we were going to experience when we got to Romania.'

The convoy headed south from Wrexham receiving an incredible reception everywhere it went. Operators at the Dartford Tunnel waved them through the tollgates without charging, P&O Ferries supplied a free meal on the ferry across the Channel, and throughout Germany they were given free fuel because they were taking aid to Romania. On the streets they often caused a stir as people stopped and stared at them, and other lorry drivers frequently acknowledged the convoy with the blast of a horn and a friendly wave.

Once in Hungary they were quick to realise the country was in quite a mess and the police had very little control, so the convoy became a law unto themselves! With no motorway systems and hundreds of small junctions, a familiar call on the radios became 'Box it up'. Each truck had its own radio and when the leader approached traffic-lights, the driver would advise them to 'box it up' by closing within a foot of each other, nose to tail, and driving straight through. And so the convoy slowly moved through Hungary, humorous radio calls building up their morale as they began the descent into Romania.

Throughout the whole journey the team had feared an accident would cast a dark shadow over the trip. As darkness fell on the Saturday their nightmare became reality. Just after entering the capital, Budapest, the ROR juggernaut leading the way screeched to a halt. Driver John Kight broke the news that the convoy was stuck because the bridge ahead was too low to negotiate. Two dreadful hours followed. The co-drivers leapt down from their cabs carrying torches to help the trucks back up along the three miles of winding roads in the pitch dark.

Almost at once a car skidded round a corner on ice and crashed into a stationary van. The potential for a very nasty accident was increasing by the minute. Surprisingly, help came in the form of a shabby Trabant car with flashing roof lights. The clapped-out vehicle pulled up and a smiley chap called Rudi climbed out to offer his assistance. 'He appeared out of nowhere and was like an angel,' Dave recalled. Rudi proceeded to use his vehicle like a New York squad car, forcing the oncoming traffic that was flying round the corner at them into taking some notice of the danger ahead. Rudi helped them to turn the trucks round in the road to save them reversing, and led them through the town and to a little place in Budapest where they could stay for the night.

Next morning they enlisted the help of 'the best taxi driver in town' to guide them out of the city, avoiding low bridges and any other potentially hazardous obstacles.

Right from the start they grasped the need for a healthy team spirit. At the heart of this was a focus on the Christian faith that was so central to the lives of the four men who formed the initial team. Before hitting the road each morning they would begin with a briefing followed by a short talk and prayer led by Clive Coleclough. Clive is a Justice of the Peace from Wrexham who was the unofficial 'spiritual adviser' on the trip (and is now a member of the Samaritan's Purse UK board). 'We were a bunch of very different characters,' explained Dave. 'We were from all sorts of walks of life, and soon realised everyone had different needs. It was all new to us, but we had to learn fast how to manage a team of amazingly different people who'd never met until a few weeks before.' A sense of humour was essential for relieving tension and keeping them going when everyone felt completely exhausted.

Dave and Dai headed up the team, and, with hindsight, are the first to admit that not all the decisions they made were the best. However, it was a new role for them, and they were learning as they went along. 'By the time we arrived in Romania, we'd learnt that you fuel all the trucks at the same time, keep them together, and make sure everyone tows the line. It took a lot of fun, and a lot of frustration to make these discoveries,' Dave admitted.

Problems hit as they arrived at the Hungarian–Romanian border. Hungarian border guards were particularly awkward, apparently angered that the aid was going to Romania when their own country had desperate needs too. 'Why you no bring us aid?' grunted one guard. Their resentment was understandable. Romania was under the media spotlight but Hungary, too, was poor and bleak. There was no evidence of Christmas celebrations for the Hungarians and yet everyone was heading to Romania.

Lengthy deliberations ensued, resulting in Operation Christmas Child offering the guards 'gifts' of paracetamol tablets, biscuits and chocolate. The convoy eventually crossed the Romanian border on the morning of Monday December 17. In Dave's words, it was 'like driving through a quarry at night, with loads of potholes and no street lights'. Traffic was minimal, except for horse-drawn carts jingling along unlit streets without warning lights. At petrol stations cars were queuing to wait for fuel, sometimes as far as three miles. The guide informed Dave, 'Here, people waiting all weekend for petrol.'

As soon as the sun came up they were hit with shock at this new culture. Reporter Paul Wilcox likened it to 'a scene straight out of George Orwell's *1984*'. The shops were stripped bare, apart from champagne and empty pickle jars. The place smelled terrible and they suddenly felt desperately insecure. 'We realised we were on our own and it felt terrible,' Dave admitted. 'I don't know how people coped in these areas without God to trust in.'

A meeting that evening at the Second Baptist Church in Oradea opened their eyes to the spiritual hunger that pervaded the country. Operation Christmas Child volunteers began handing out small gifts and food to the crowds that surrounded them, but outside the church a hand slipped through the window of the chase car that led the convoy. A shy voice whispered fearfully, 'Please, have you just one Bible?' They had lived through a spiritual famine during the Communist reign of the past 50 years, and this was a cry from the heart.

That night Dave had a secret rendezvous with his contacts. The Romanians were piling on pressure to take control of the supplies themselves, but Dave was adamant. Operation Christmas Child had agreed to deliver the aid personally, not least to ensure that it didn't find its way on to the black market.

Nothing could have prepared the Operation Christmas Child team for the horror that awaited them when they arrived at the first orphanage. Driving through impoverished peasant farms and villages, the landscape threw them back a couple of generations. The gates of the orphanage were obstructed by a crowd of gypsies, desperate to get their hands on the supplies so they could sell them on. Determined to reach the children, the volunteers climbed out of the trucks, filled their arms with shoeboxes and pushed their way into the muddy grey courtyard. As they looked up, they saw a huddle of gaunt-faced children staring blankly at them through a barred window ahead.

A deathly quiet hung over the first room they entered, disturbed only by the clicking noise of the children grinding their own teeth out of boredom. Urine-soaked cots and the solitary lavatory for more than a hundred children released an unbearable stench throughout the building. Each door that was opened revealed another room full of children starved of love and affection. They looked like little moon people: they had never seen a toy in their lives and just sat staring into space. One member of the convoy remarked, 'It was amazing that they were even alive.'

The tough truck drivers were reduced to tears and many were forced to leave the room, overwhelmed by an atrocity they could never have imagined. They would go outside and build each other up before going back in again, but all felt emotionally wrecked.

In an attempt to build up a massive land army, Nicolae Ceausescu had insisted that every woman have at least four babies. But the regime he had subjected them to meant that the women couldn't afford to support the children and so the orphanage system came into effect. Thousands of little lives were institutionalised in these houses of horror while the 'best' were weeded out and directed into prostitution by the Securitate.

On the day Operation Christmas Child visited that orphanage, a small flicker of light shone into the dark lives of these horribly neglected children. The moment the children began receiving their parcels was wonderful. The atmosphere in the room burst into life. Drab, emotionless and vacant faces were transformed with smiles and laughter. Some were too overwhelmed to react, but others ran to embrace, kiss, and cuddle the volunteers. A rocking horse was placed in the middle of one room and the children touched and smiled and stroked the wooden horse. Some didn't know what it meant to play, and sitting on the horse was the first experience of what it felt like to enjoy life.

Moments of sad comedy invaded the excitement. Some little children were intrigued by sweet smelling packages and were found chewing on bars of soap. Others were happily sucking on tubes of toothpaste.

The staff that looked after the children were paid a few pence per week and had very few resources, but despite this they wanted to feed the drivers. It was food that back home the drivers wouldn't have even given to pigs, but the willingness of the Romanians to give what they had amazed the team and they made an effort to return the generosity with gratitude. The smell was awful and the plates dirty, but as one of the team said, 'We've given thanks for this food, we'd better sit and eat it.'

As they got back into the trucks they began to build each other up for the next job. It was a soul-destroying mission and they were all struggling. Some were filled with anger at the corruption and injustice. Why have the rich got all the money? Why are these kids suffering? Why is the government not doing anything? Look at Ceausescu's palace – what's gone wrong? As they left the orphanage, gypsies thronged round the trucks, hoping to get something for themselves. A nuisance, even a danger, to the convoy, the drivers revved up the engines to bypass them quickly. But then it struck them. They were poor too. They weren't terrible people. Just like the kids in the orphanage, they desperately needed to be loved and to share in Christmas. Dave's four-year-old daughter, Sarah, had put a tatty doll in her daddy's bag as he left. As they handed out gifts to the gypsies, a little girl caught Dave's eye. Her face was grubby and her clothes in tatters, but something in him thought this was just the kind of girl Sarah would like to give her doll to.

A prime concern for Dave was to ensure that the aid made it to those who needed it most. In the weeks of preparation they had made contact with Christians in Romania and arranged meetings with people they could trust.

A spectacular journey over the Caucasus mountain range led them down into the city of Cluj. Their instructions were to meet a man who would be standing beside a road sign on the outskirts of the town at a certain time. He was Liviu Balas, a contact given to Dave by Gary Cox, who runs the Bristol-based aid charity Eurovangelism. It was Liviu, complete with his huge beard, who would meet them each day on the side of the road at a pre-arranged location to give them directions to the next place of need. He'd given his life to working for these desperate Romanian kids and set up an organisation called Ecce Homo, Latin for 'Behold the Man'. Dave said, 'He is one of the most amazing guys I ever met working in that country. He was able to set us in just the right direction.'

Cluj Hospital was a crumbling building where dingy corridors led to decaying wards. The building itself needed demolition, but the horror stories that were waiting inside were even more disturbing. One doctor told how a week earlier he had performed a Caesarean section without anaesthetic. Worse still, the scalpels were so old and blunt that a stabbing action had to be used to make an incision.

The men rolled up their sleeves and helped in any way they could, from unloading medical supplies and delivering them to different departments, to helping set up a new cardiac unit. Countless lives were saved through that one delivery alone.

As they left Romania, plans to return were already starting to form in Dave's mind. There was much to think about, many dreams for the future, so much to do. As the convoy neared Wrexham, they turned the radio on to hear the familiar strains of Marcher Sound. Chris Rea's 'Driving home for Christmas' was played especially for them and it's a tune that will always provoke special memories for that very first team.

Just before entering their hometown, the trucks stopped. Everyone grouped together and said their goodbyes. They'd experienced something together that would make its own mark on each of their lives. Emotions were highly charged. Tough guys who had been thrown together at the beginning, with all their differences and foibles, now shared a very deep bond. There was something there that they didn't want to lose. Their goodbyes over, they were ready to make their way to the warehouse to receive a hero's welcome and be reunited with family and friends.

They returned to Wrexham just a couple of days before Christmas and the contrast with Romania could not have been starker. Dave remembers being irritated at a local supermarket: 'People were squabbling about what they were going to get, like what size of turkey. I felt like shouting, "Look, people in Romania have nothing. Stop arguing."' Each one of them found it a struggle to cope with the emotional pressure as they gave and received presents on Christmas Day. Dave admitted, 'After what we'd experienced my mind kept going back, and blank.' It took him a while to adjust, but says it is something he's better able to cope with now: 'I don't think it gets any easier, though. The day I get blasé about it, I'll pack it all in.'

Over a decade later, Dave still retains a deep level of personal involvement in the work, and his compassion for suffering children is as strong as ever. The work of Operation Christmas Child has gone from strength to strength, bringing love and happiness to millions of children. Much has happened since those early days in Wrexham, and Operation Christmas Child is now part of the international charity Samaritan's Purse. It delivers aid – and the message of hope that is found in Jesus Christ – to victims of poverty, natural disaster and war around the world.

But what drove Dave to give what he had to those who have nothing? Was he always heading towards the role of 'Father Christmas' to tens of thousands of children? His former headmaster obviously didn't think so! Dave recalls being told, 'Cooke, you'll never achieve anything!' before being promptly told to leave the premises for good. It's amazing what God can do with a person when he gets hold of a life and chooses to use it for good.

This chapter is taken from *Love In A Box* by Emma Carswell, published by Paternoster, 2001.

HODDER & STOUGHTON

David Westlake is youth director of Tearfund.
His book, *Outwardly Active*, like his acclaimed
Upwardly Mobile, turns the cosy traditional
approach to the Christian life on its head.

First published in Great Britain in 2001

10 9 8 7 6 5 4 3 2 1

British Library Cataloguing-in-Publication Data
A record for this book is available from the British Library

ISBN 0 340 78556 X
Hodder & Stoughton
A Division of Hodder Headline Ltd
338 Euston Road
London NW1 3BH

Words, Works and Wonders

by David Westlake

Therefore I glory in Christ Jesus in my service to God. I will not venture to speak of anything except what Christ has accomplished through me in leading the Gentiles to obey God by what I have said and done – by the power of signs and miracles, through the power of the Spirit. So from Jerusalem all the way round to Illyricum, I have fully proclaimed the gospel of Christ. It has always been my ambition to preach the gospel where Christ was not known, so that I would not be building on someone else's foundation. Rather, as it is written: 'Those who were not told about him will see, and those who have not heard will understand.' This is why I have often been hindered from coming to you (Romans 15:17–22).

The passage above finds Paul chewing the fat with a few evangelism anoraks keen to find out some of his top tips. According to this reply, Paul's goal of quality evangelism has been fully achieved and has been executed through the words he has spoken, the deeds he has done and the power of the Holy Spirit at work. If you happen to be a fan of the King James version of the Bible, you'll see that the translation lists as the three prongs of Paul's evangelistic strategy 'words . . . works . . . and wonders'. And as Paul seemed to do OK for himself, I wonder whether we too might be able to pick up a few tips from his particular model.

For too long we in the church have grasped the wrong end of this particular strategic stick. We have considered words, works and wonders as elements to be kept separate from each other. And this is quite handy, as it has allowed us to develop a taste for a particular style without feeling guilty at our lack of adventure. So we have the option of putting all our interests in the art of delivering a good gospel message, or we search long and hard for the perfect tract, one that will have people falling to their knees at the quickest of readings. Or we might opt for the works side of things, where we take on the role of unqualified and unpaid social workers. No other form of communication about Jesus is permitted than works of compassion, which can get a little tricky once people start to ask questions about why we behave in a certain way. Or we can choose to be real 'signs and wonders' merchants, believing in the power of the Holy Spirit above all others to change lives. Here we might take on the role of entertainer, believing that people need nothing more than to see something truly 'WOW' in order to secure their belief. But you know what? Separating them out like that doesn't do anyone any favours, least of all the very people we're trying to reach. Yet if we can hold them together, if we can discover the knack of being able to hold the three seemingly opposing styles in harmony, much as Paul did, then the results could be truly spectacular.

Words

I once had a job as a barman in a cocktail bar close to London's business centre. It was close to St Paul's, and at the time I was pleased enough that I'd managed to find work in so trendy a place – one with a neon sign and everything. Being full of my usual spiritual zeal and earnestness I'd made a number of pledges to God before starting my first shift. On leaving that evening, I was forced back to the boardroom of my mind to renegotiate some of my earlier promises. After just a few hours I was convinced that there was no possible chance of me being successfully able to tell the people who worked there about my faith. And as for substituting gospel tracts for those napkins on which the drinks were placed – well, that would clearly have not only got me fired but publicly lynched too. You see, the people I was now working with were serious non-Christians. And they were very good at it.

After a few weeks of working there I was travelling home on the train one night feeling guilty about my poor performance, especially as the old desire to do something positive among my colleagues had resurfaced. I felt God tell me simply to tell the truth, which was an odd thing as I wouldn't have said that I'd exactly been lying while I'd been working there. But as I thought about it things became a little clearer. Being a city bar it was closed over the weekend so there was an element of debrief about the first shift on Monday. There people would go through their weekends, picking out the juicy bits and discarding the moments of tedium. When it came to my turn I realised that I tended to big up the Saturday activities and play down those that occurred on a Sunday. I'd say things like 'Yeah, Sunday was great . . . really relaxing to be with the family . . .' Which was true. But not completely true. My weekend story should have included a closing line about how much I had (or hadn't) enjoyed church on Sunday night but somehow my voice always seemed to trail off before I got to that point. Which was convenient.

So I decided to change my ways and, whenever they asked me questions, to tell the truth. This seemed to work just fine, as for a few days people seemed to have lost their desire to talk

to me, but one afternoon their shyness van-
ished.

'Where have you been?' asked Sarah, one of
the other bar staff.

I had been doing what I usually did, which
was to go up to St Paul's Cathedral and have a
quiet time in one of the side chapels. So I told
her where I'd been.

'Oh it's lovely up there. Did you do the
whole tourist thing and take a tour?'

'Um', I said, 'not quite'.

And I explained about my time spent praying and reading my Bible. She looked at me
blankly and then asked me the last question I
had expected.

'Why do you pray?'

I couldn't think of a single reason. Eventually
I mumbled something about how I felt that it
helped, how I thought it was a good thing for
me to be doing. She was interested and asked
me what I prayed. I told her how I covered
things like asking God for guidance and forgiveness, about praying for family, friends and
work colleagues.

'So do you pray for us, then?'

'Yeah'.

'What do you pray?'

Again I gave another spectacularly unim-
pressive answer, as insipid words like 'nice',
'happy' and 'good' dribbled out of my mouth. I
felt like the world's worst evangelist and had a

sudden, frighteningly clear mental image of Billy Graham playing football with my head. But at least Sarah seemed interested, and she kept on coming up to me throughout the rest of the afternoon and evening to ask me further 'what' and 'how' and 'why' questions about my not-so-secret religious side.

She'd told others, too, and they quickly took an interest in things, which I thought was just a bit unfair: I was in this wretched deal with God whereby I had to answer if they asked. So I regularly volunteered to go down to the cellar to change the barrels just so that I could get some peace and quiet and pretend to be hiding my faith again.

Later, when the bar was packed, Sarah was carrying on her quick-fire questions about my faith as the song that had been playing came to an end. A sudden lull came over the bar just as she was halfway through her question:

'So David, are you one of those Christians that doesn't believe in sex?'

Everyone turned to look at me. I closed my eyes and wished for a miracle that would transport me far, far away.

* * *

When I had started the job hardly any of the staff had ever met a Christian. When I left I'd been able to talk to most of them and hand out a few bibles. Why? Because our words matter, and when we commit to being real with people and telling the truth, God's Kingdom comes a little nearer. Making that pact with God worked for me because I finally realised that talking about God to people who hardly knew him was not about slipping into a sales pitch, not about turning up the charm in an effort to schmooze someone into the Kingdom. Instead, it was simply about being honest.

Works

Let's get this straight: by 'works' I don't mean 'effort'. We cannot sweat, squeeze or strain people into God's Kingdom any more than we can argue them in. By 'works' I mean deeds of compassion, actions that speak louder than words, behaviour that takes its lead from Jesus' actions. Strangely, we have to be explicit about this, as the church in the West has struggled to get to grips with the idea that works of compassion are of themselves a decent evangelistic tool. We've come across all confused when others have suggested that to feed the hungry or clothe the poor is in itself an act that brings the Kingdom of God closer to people. Sadly, unless the works have been accompanied by a 'let me tell you about Jesus' line, we've suspected that we've been wasting our time. But try telling that to Christians in certain developing countries and they'd look at you like you're deranged. For many who face poverty so frequently and in such severity, it is blindingly obvious that if the hungry are fed then God's good news is being preached. If people are homeless then the good news of Jesus surely is that they have somewhere to live.

In attempting to separate works from spreading the news of Jesus, we've got into evangelism that has little to do with people's personal needs, as well as meeting people's personal needs in a way that is wholly unrelated to evangelism. Both of these strike me as a shame, especially when I consider the kind of work that a friend of mine does with long-term unemployed people in a large city. This project has the highest success rate of any of its kind in the country, and has been patted on the back by the government and told that it is a model project. How? Because they don't only offer job-related training, but by forming relationships they invest in every single person who joins them so that their confidence grows in every area of their lives. This means they wind up talking to people about all manner of issues, from debt to family, education to parenting, and at every turn try to offer quality relationships that can make a difference. It's wonderful to see Christians work together in this way, but deep down perhaps we all know that there are some who would question whether a project as committed and generous as this really is evangelistic. Why? Because there are no words being used, no tracts being handed out at the start of each course.

I once met some members of a university Christian Union who had recently hit on success with their annual mission. Like many CUs, they felt that they wanted to do something each year to reach out and spread the good news among their fellow students. For years they had hired in the big-name evangelist and the band, handed out flyers in the daytime and held gigs and debates in the evenings, and while things had worked just fine, one year they decided to ring the changes and opt for something completely different. So they chose a specific developing country, found out about projects within the country that were working with the poorest people, and generally got themselves well acquainted with the specific problems and potential solutions for the people in need. Next they produced a range of T-shirts, postcards and so on and launched a university-wide campaign to help raise both funds and awareness about the plight of the people. The campaign ran for a week and involved loads of people – only a few of whom were Christians – and made a huge impact on campus life. At the end of each day all those involved would go back to the bar and talk things over, plan for the next day and generally unwind. By the end of the week-long mission the CU saw more people become Christians than through the previous three missions combined. Why? Because the Christians stopped being known as people who talked and started to be known as people who did.

[Now, this section on works has deliberately been kept a little on the short side: not because it all sounds like a bit too much hard graft, but due to the simple fact that all my ideas got used up in *Upwardly Mobile*, a book that deals with the theme in greater depth.]

Problems and Solutions

You see, sometimes this evangelism thing all feels too impersonal. It's as if we have to drop our personality – our likes, dislikes, opinions and character – and start to spout the party line. At times I've felt as if, midway through a quiet drink with a friend, I ought to have put down my pint, adopted a pleasant yet serious expression and 'got down to business' by explaining the real reason for my being there. And what if my real reason for being there was because I wanted to hang out with a friend? Not good enough: at times it feels like the real reason for socialising with non-Christians is so that they can become Christians. Well, I'm sorry, but that won't do. If all our friendships have a 'save by' date on them, if all our social gatherings need to taper expertly to a moment where we can dim the lights, down the music and whisper sweet spiritual nothings in our friend's ear, then count me out. Come to think of it, you could probably count out Jesus, Paul and the early church, too: for them, relationships were valid in themselves. They were neither conditional on progress nor fake about truth. Yes, Jesus told his disciples to shake the dust and all that, but that was more about relationships that had failed to take off than friends who were unwilling to listen. At the end of the day, there's got to be a way that I can show, tell and inspire people about the God I love without having to leave my personality at the door. Hasn't there?

Wonders

As a product it's not hard to see some of the flaws present within Christianity. Why, by the process of a simple tweak here and a nip and tuck there, the whole thing could have so much more pzazz, be far easier to handle and feel so much more comfortable. If only we could make it so that regular Christian life was like the isolated pockets of fired-up frenzy we all love so much when it comes round to the annual Christian festival. There our doubts fly away, our spirits soar and our consciences wash a whiter shade of white. There's a miracle at the end of every meeting, a tale of victory being told at every queue and just enough heroes up on the platform to wow, sparkle and give us all something to aim for. Life at these times is easy, far easier than the harsh reality of home. There the miracles certainly are not waiting behind every closed door, and the supermarkets are most certainly not the venues for powerful moves of the Holy Spirit. We may have been used to seeing wonderful moves of God at the festival, but as soon as we're back home the idea of seeing God's power in action in any place other than the church can be frankly odd.

It's sad to admit it, but the whole area of wonders – works of the Holy Spirit – is yet another that we have pensioned off away from the subject of everyday evangelism. We might admit to it working for a few individuals up there on the platform, but when it comes to us, most often we find the prospect of praying for a miracle in the middle of the pub nothing short of embarrassing.

Once, when I was involved in a church working in one of the more deprived areas of

London, there was a time when we'd get regular visits to our outreach evenings from a particularly rough group of lads. They'd been in and out of police custody, and most had spent time in young offenders' institutions. Naturally they scared the life out of me. One particular night they turned up and were being unusually aggressive. Being a generous and balanced leader, I decided to send someone else over to deal with them, and from my position cowering behind a bench I watched as two of the more petite women on the team went up to them. They talked, but I couldn't hear their precise words. As I watched I saw one of the women raise her hand, looking as if she was about to slap one of the lads. Visions of a horribly quick and one-sided fight flashed across my mind, and I decided that there was nothing for it but for me to step in and offer myself as a martyr. Thankfully my blood wasn't needed that day: by the time I had walked across, the woman had prayed for one of the biggest lads, who swooned a bit and then fell over. His friends looked on, not knowing whether to fight, laugh or run off.

'That was fantastic!' he said after a few seconds on the floor. 'What was it?'

'That', said the woman, 'was God.'

All his friends made gentle 'oooooh' noises and looked back at their mate.

'Do it again,' came his reply.

Faced with the option of having him back up and pushing people about, getting the lad dosed up on the Holy Spirit for the night seemed like a very attractive option, even if it felt a little bit like a side-show attraction. After he'd been up and down a couple of times his mates wanted to have a go too, and by the time the hour was up they had all 'had a dose', as they put it.

And they came back. Week after week they turned up to the meetings, and we got to know them. Their stories were told and we began to understand a little of what they had been through. It might not have been the most comfortable of experiences at first, but it brought home the message to all of us in the church: that sometimes we simply have to get on with the business of trusting God and expect him to move in power. Simple.

Perhaps it is this type of risk, this danger of suffering extreme embarrassment, that prevents us from signing up fully to the workings of the Holy Spirit. After all, it could so easily have gone horribly wrong for my friend as she started to pray for the tough lad: nothing might have happened to him and the whole relationship would have taken a slide even further back down the hill. But isn't that the point? If we want to see God do amazing things, doesn't it make sense that we put ourselves in positions where we are fully dependent on him to work?

Isn't it simply a matter of saying something like 'Can I pray for you?' They can only say 'no'. Whether it 'works' or not is up to God, and it's bound to get a few questions going.

Having spent a few weeks coming to our outreach evenings in a local pub, eventually the lads wanted to come along to our church services. Which was interesting. As soon as they saw the ministry going on at the end of the service they started to get excited. 'That bloke just punched that woman!' they'd shout from the back. It took some explaining to make it clear that what was going on was not people hitting each other but God moving in much the same way as he had when the lads themselves had fallen over. 'So can we go and watch?'

The thought of seven colossal lads from Deptford crowding around someone receiving ministry somehow didn't quite seem to fit with the established protocol, but when I started to um and ah about their request they complained that it was obviously a fake. So they went up and watched. And they commented. Loudly. 'Go on, then', they'd tell the person who was getting ready to do the praying, 'knock him out.' Then, turning to the person who had come up for ministry, they'd offer a comforting, 'Don't worry, it's only God.'

Even looking back to those days now. I'm tempted to think of the circumstances as odd: seven hard lads staring at people during ministry, challenging people to 'hit them with God' and generally experiencing the power of the Holy Spirit long before they knew anything about being a Christian. But why should it feel odd? Why should that be unusual? Surely it's a shame that we've removed wonders from our evangelism, reserving them as treats not to be opened until a contract has been signed. And isn't this the heart of the problem with our approach to evangelism: that we have managed to isolate, extract and sanitise the whole process. We've made it into a programme, we've written a script and we've developed a technique. Worst of all, we've moved the whole deal far, far away from the essential truth: that evangelism is about introducing people to a relationship with Jesus. Paul did that any way he could – through words, works and wonders – but for us some of these aspects have become strangers.

It wasn't only Paul who adopted a multi-faceted, relationship-oriented approach to spreading the gospel. It doesn't take that long spent flicking through the book of Acts to work out that the growth of the early church was based on a similar foundation:

They devoted themselves to the apostles' teach-ing and to the fellowship, to the breaking of bread and to prayer. Everyone was filled with awe, and many wonders and miraculous signs were done by the apostles. All the believers were together and had everything in common. Selling their possessions and goods, they gave to anyone as he had need. Every day they continued to meet together in the temple courts. They broke bread in their homes and ate together with glad and sincere hearts, praising God and enjoying the favour of all the people. And the Lord added to their number daily those who were being saved (Acts 2:42–7).

Discussion, sacrificial living and miracles: three core ingredients that fertilised the growth of the early church. Somehow they managed to combine the more formal platform-based evangelistic activities with their own personal responsibilities, and perhaps we too could do with learning how to do the same. It can be too easy for us to switch off and consider that evangelism is either something that other people – other more gifted public speakers – do for us or something that we do only when we have to, but such a methodology fits neither Jesus' model nor Paul's.

If we're going to be really honest with ourselves here we ought to admit that it is in this area of personal evangelism that we should be seeing the most growth. Sure, the big events and missions are still important and will bring fresh people into contact and relationship with Jesus, but the church's best chance of growth surely lies with us, the majority. Whether together or on our own, we have the potential for following Paul's lead and relying on all three aspects of evangelism. Instead of scheduling in monthly 'Let me tell you about why you're going to hell' type conversations with our acquaintances, we can start to live lives that get people asking questions. Being honest in our replies will add further layers to the relationship, and relying on God to deliver all that flash stuff – well, doesn't that relieve the pressure from us just a little?

And what are we evangelising for, anyway? Is it for a conversion? Are we in it for the head-count, to see how many contracts we can get signed in a certain period of time? Or are we following Jesus' model, are we aiming to produce disciples, people who have a deepening relationship with Jesus? Of course, if we're choosing to offer this second option it will take a whole lot more time and is best not taught from a textbook but shown by example. Deciding to commit to quality relationships with people reframes our whole outlook on evangelism: out goes the emphasis on quantity and in comes a new commitment to quality; we say goodbye to the quick fix and welcome the search for the truth; we put down our defences and we welcome people to get to know the real us.

Case study

Caroline was one of those good Christians who grew up in a good Christian home, went to a good Christian church and lived an altogether good Christian life. She didn't drink, smoke, flirt outrageously or take her faith too lightly. She was a model member of the church youth group, one the leaders lost no sleep about. And then she left. No warning. No goodbyes, just a disappearance. Of course, she was still around, bumping into people at school and at the shops on a Saturday afternoon, but as far as church was concerned – well, it was as if it had never happened. People from the group tried to get in touch. They wanted to find out what was wrong and whether they could do anything to help her through this crisis of faith, but she hung up their calls, binned their e-mails or stared blankly past their concerned frowns.

If they could have seen her diaries they would have given up the search for answers: within the pages was a stream of bitterness and frustration, the real story about a faith that had been based on nothing more than feelings. One day she had realised something profound: that the

feelings were no longer there. So she did
the only thing that made sense and cut
God out of her life.

Years went by, and occasional conversations with ex-church members became
less and less frequent. Strangely, she
began to find herself thinking about going
back. Was her faith based completely on
feelings? Wasn't there the chance that just
one small particle had been based on
something true? Might part of it have
been something other than an illusion?

While most of the people she bumped
into from church still looked awkward,
there were a couple of people who had
stuck by her throughout her years away
from church and God. These had been the
only two who hadn't tried to persuade
her to go back, the only ones who had
allowed her to rant and rave about all the
things she was struggling with. One summer they invited her on holiday with
them: it was a church affair but if she went
along she would be doing them a favour
by helping out with some of the jobs they
had to do there. She joined them and
found herself surprised at how much fun
she was having. She was amazed at how
the new people she met were interested in
her, about how they didn't judge or

assume things about her. So she hung around the church meetings that were taking place on the camp, eyeing the proceedings up, wary of getting caught in the emotional whirl again. No one was fussed whether she went in or not, and neither of her friends questioned her about whether she was coming back to church. On the last day, quietly, without anyone knowing, she prayed again for the first time in years. She asked God for help. That night she went to sleep feeling, for the first time ever, like she was coming home.

This chapter is taken from *Outwardly Active: Evangelism As Jesus Did It*, published by Hodder & Stoughton, 2001.

CARE FOR THE FAMILY

Rob Parsons is an international speaker on business and family issues. He has spoken to more than 300,000 people in seminars around the world and his books, including best-sellers such as *The Sixty-Minute Father* and *The Sixty-Minute Marriage*, have sold approaching half a million copies in ten languages.

Don't Lose Heart

by Rob Parsons

Some time ago now a Canadian friend sent me an account of an event that occurred when he was a child.

Late December in northern Ontario, Canada, is traditionally cold and snowy. I remember those winters so well but, in particular, my mind goes back almost forty years to a Christmas in 1958.

Several miles from our home, deep in the country, was an isolated dwelling inhabited by an old recluse called Percy. Percy was something of a local mystery. Most adults found it easier to ignore him and most kids were in awe of him. Rumour had it that if he caught you within a mile of his place you would disappear forever.

My parents had always been generous people and if my father was scared of Percy he never showed it. In fact every Christmas Eve he trudged through the woods to Percy's cottage to give him some Christmas gifts and just, as he put it, 'to let the old boy know somebody cares.'

December 24 1958 stands out clearly in my
mind. New snow had blanketed our valley the
night before when the weather had turned clear
and cold. I came downstairs and found my father
making breakfast beside the old stove. He turned
to me: 'In a moment I'm going to make my trip to
Percy's place. Would you like to come with me?'

I said I'd go.

Dad and I set off and after 30 minutes or so my
father pointed to a thin wisp of smoke curling up
from the centre of the wood. We waded through
knee-deep snowdrifts and finally knocked on
Percy's door.

It was not opened by a monster but by an old
man with holes in his clothes and a gruff voice
that welcomed us in. We entered a one-roomed
house that had seen better days and was filled
with the smell of a hardwood fire and the unmistakable waft of body odour and old tobacco. Dad
set the bags of groceries we had hauled through
the wood on to a sticky oilcloth-covered table,
near where Percy invited us to sit.

Percy and Dad made small talk, discussing the
recent turn in the weather and whether there
would be enough wood to last the winter. After
all the local topics had been well covered Dad
said, 'Well, Percy, Christmas is here again and
our family just wanted you to have a few groceries as our gift to you. You know, Percy,
Christmas is important to us because of the birth
of Christ.'

And then my young eyes saw something that I have never forgotten. A single tear began to roll down Percy's face and into his thick bushy beard. He quickly brushed it away with the back of a dirty hand as he mumbled his thanks. My father said that it was time we were going and shook Percy's hand as we rose and made for the door. Just as we were about to step out into the snow Percy reached out and touched my father's arm. 'Don', he said, ' you are a bearer of hope.'

I will never forget that scene, for, in a moment of time on December 24, I was taught a great lesson: God softens grizzled old hearts through the kind acts of his people. That was to be the last Christmas Eve journey my father made, for Percy died early the following year.

I have thought so much about that story. What does it mean to be 'a bearer of hope'? I think it means that we bring people the news that life can change; we bring to people the promise of a better tomorrow. For that to happen it is vital that we ourselves do not lose heart. It's quite a challenge. The world is filled with people who have done just that. I have sometimes seen it in the eyes of somebody who has just lost their job: it's almost as if they have been robbed of dignity itself; sometimes they exhibit similar symptoms to grief at the loss of a loved one. I have seen it in the creeping despair of a parent who is consumed with worry over a teenager, and I have sometimes observed it in a church leader who can simply take no more.

To lose heart is often a precursor to losing life itself, for we lose the very will to live. And I have often seen those eyes of despair in the faces of the followers of Jesus. Somebody, some circumstance, or just the sheer accumulation of years of hardship has caused them to lose heart.

I once lost heart in dramatic fashion. I noticed that our local leisure club was to hold a Tuesday 'keep-fit' evening. I should have deduced from the title that it was designed for those who wanted to retain what they had already achieved, rather than for those for whom the concept was only a dream. That detail was lost on me and I went. My son lent me a pair of trainers and I found a pair of tracksuit bottoms that I last used in form five at school. They seemed to have shrunk a little, but nevertheless I donned the kit and set off.

The room was full. I have never seen such tiny waists and so much Lycra concentrated into such a small floor area. These creatures were rippling fitness. The instructor introduced herself and I stood listening whilst vainly trying to hold my stomach in, and, at the same time, attempting to retrieve the cord of my joggers, which had disappeared into the waistband.

She distributed tasks around the room and left me until last. It seemed she had decided I needed a little personal tuition. She told me she wanted to test my basic fitness before launching me on the terrors that most of the other Lycra wearers were now engaged in. She took my pulse and then asked me to leap up and down on what looked like a small orange box. I kept this up for all of a minute and then, seeing the colour in my face, and fearing the worst, she asked me to stop. She waited a short while and then took my pulse again. Apparently if one is reasonably fit one's pulse returns to normal within two to three minutes. Mine came back on the following Thursday afternoon.

I had literally lost heart. If you had asked me to perform the simplest of functions when I had got off the orange box I couldn't have. With all the good will in the world *there was nothing left to give.*

Over the years I have observed and at times experienced some of the things that cause us to lose heart. I want to mention two in particular.

The power of the past

The first is being dogged by the past. Dianne and I were engaged when I was 21. I had just finished college and was penniless. That wouldn't have been such a problem if I hadn't needed to buy an engagement ring. Now, if I were counselling my own children in that situation, I would advise that they get a job and save for the ring, and, in so doing, they would make the experience more precious and more meaningful. It's good advice but it discounts the irrationality of love. I went to my bank manager.

Since that fateful day I have often had to deal with bank managers, but in those days I was a trifle naïve in such matters. I'm not sure what I expected, but perhaps thought he might say, 'In love! How splendid! A penniless student – ideal! How much would you like?' Instead he smiled at me. It wasn't a warm, encouraging smile – rather the forced, wind-like smile of one who was about to say, 'If you don't get out of my bank fast, I'll call security.'

I borrowed the money elsewhere and we bought a second-hand ring. One year later we bought a wedding band in a discount jeweller's, and we were married. Shortly after I qualified as a lawyer I bought Dianne an eternity ring. Those rings held such memories for us.

Just after our 25th wedding anniversary we were on holiday with our children and some friends. The rest of us had been in the sea for some time when Dianne joined us. And then it happened. She threw a ball to me and suddenly something flashed in the sunlight. I watched as three rings, as if in slow motion, left Dianne's hand. They seemed to hover in the air for a moment and then disappeared into the sea. At the same time she shouted 'My rings!' and I saw a look of utter grief on her face. I know that in the great sweep of life there are things a lot bigger than losing a little jewellery, but it was more than that: it was the memories, the emotion that those things held – and they were gone.

Of course, we searched, but the sea was rough and our efforts were futile. For days afterwards I walked along the edge of the water half expecting to see them lying there, waiting to be reclaimed. We never did get those rings back. I often think of them lying somewhere, or perhaps by now they are on other hands – but they are still full of our memories. If they could talk they would tell how they have heard times of helpless laughter and of crying that seemed to come from the very soul. In short, they hold the memories of two lives, each with successes and failures. If I am wise I will learn lessons from that past but in another sense I must let go of it and move on.

Our yesterdays have a strange power over us. One way they can cause us to lose heart is because we believe the future could never be as good as the past. As we look back it seems the summers were hotter, the trains more reliable and life better in almost every way. In such a mood we can yearn for our church to be like it used to be, our teenagers to be toddlers again, and society to be as it was. Of course there may be sense in wanting those things, but the book of Ecclesiastes has in it a fascinating warning: 'Do not say, "Why were the old days better than these?" For it is not wise to ask such questions' (Ecclesiastes 7:10). The past can trap us because it seems so good; we are tied to it. We refuse to face tomorrow because the memories of yesterday are so sweet.

Many a church leader is weary of people telling him or her how wonderful church used to be; many a child is tired of a parent reminding her how perfect her sister was when she was that age; and lots of people never move into new experiences because in their hearts they continually hanker after 'how it used to be'. The past may have been wonderful, but usually it wasn't as great as our memory makes out, and in any event *it is still the past*. Mark Twain said 'Plan for the future, it's where you're going to spend the rest of your life.'

But there is another problem of the past, and it is the opposite one. Some of us cannot face tomorrow because we are haunted by our yesterdays. With us it is not the problem of yearning for the years that have gone, but never being able to forget them. They remind us of sorrow and pain, perhaps failure and crushing disappointment. You may feel like that now. There is so much in life you would love to do but you crouch like a rabbit suddenly caught in the headlights of a car, unable to move forward or back. Because of the hurt or failure of the past you have lost the confidence to go on.

The story of the Bible is of God using ordinary men and women who achieved what they did in spite of, and not because of, what they were. Many of them had known pasts with shame and failure in them but they experienced the truth of a fascinating promise God gave Israel. That nation had known years of spiritual barrenness but he said to them: 'I will repay you for the years the locusts have eaten' (Joel 2:25).

Imagine what it was like the day the locusts came. One moment the fields were full of wheat blowing in the wind and then you heard the sound. And after the sound came the darkness, as if the sun itself had given up in the face of the devastation that swept across the land. And when they were gone there was only ruin. The preparation, the sowing, the careful tending – all wasted. The hope of the harvest was dead.

Most of us go through a time in our lives when we identify with this. The years have taken their toll of us. We look back on disappointment, failure and heartache. We believe our life has been devastated. Such a situation may come about for many reasons. We may be victims of the wrongs of others, or our own wrongs may have caused us to pay a price we

would never have imagined. It may be that illness or disappointments in our family have
consumed our thoughts and drained us of
effort. But God can change our lives: he can
restore to us the years the locust has eaten.

This does not mean that suddenly life
becomes easy, but it does mean that tomorrow
does not have to be like yesterday. The times of
darkness and nights of tears, the memories of
past failure, need not imprison us forever. This
is true even if that devastation is because we
have been foolish; even if the responsibility lies
just with us. He is a God of new beginnings.

For the past three years I have presented a
live seminar. The other day I received a letter
from a woman who had been present at one of
those events. She was a professional person, in
her mid-50s, and had only recently disclosed to
a counsellor a rape that took place when she
was 12 years old. This is part of what she wrote:

> I still struggle with the fact that I can be both
> loveable and loved, but slowly the truth dawns.
> Sometimes living has been like dying. Sometimes
> I have wanted to die. But I find at such times that
> God almost bombards me with the message that
> he loves me and values me. I now work for a
> Christian ministry and countless adults now
> approach me and tell of their own history of
> abuse and the new life they now seek. My past
> has become a gift to help bring new life to others.

And so God often does it. He takes a past that has in it only sorrow and uses it to bring joy. It is full of defeat but he uses it to lead others to victory. He redeems our yesterdays.

I was regretting the past
And fearing the future ...
Suddenly my Lord was speaking:
'MY NAME IS I AM.' He paused.
I waited. He continued.

'WHEN YOU LIVE IN THE PAST
WITH ITS MISTAKES AND REGRETS
IT IS HARD. I AM NOT THERE.
MY NAME IS NOT *I WAS*.

WHEN YOU LIVE IN THE FUTURE
WITH ITS PROBLEMS AND FEARS
IT IS HARD. I AM NOT THERE.
MY NAME IS NOT *I WILL BE*.

WHEN YOU LIVE IN THIS MOMENT
IT IS NOT HARD
I AM HERE.
MY NAME IS *I AM*.'[1]

When nothing makes sense

But even if we deal with our past there is another issue that time and time again forces us to lose heart. The clue to it is in something Paul wrote to the Christians who lived at Corinth:

'We are hard pressed on every side, but not crushed; perplexed, but not in despair; persecuted, but not abandoned; struck down, but not destroyed' (2 Corinthians 4:8–9). That's quite a list, but I think of all those difficulties the hardest to bear may have been 'perplexed'. The literal meaning is 'at a loss as to know how to go on'. When you are hard pressed you know you are in a battle, when you are persecuted you can see the enemy, being struck down is a terrible thing, but at least you know where the blow came from. But 'perplexed'?

This is a time when we don't understand what is going on. It may even be a time when it appears God has left us, let us down, or in our lowest moments seems even to have betrayed us. It could be in the area of our prayer life. We had honestly believed God was going to answer our prayers with a resounding 'Yes!' The person we prayed for was so precious and we desperately wanted him to be well. And there were so many encouraging signs. We prayed the operation would be successful and it seemed to be; we prayed through every day of the treatment, and, as time went by, we had a growing sense that all would be well. But our friend died. We accepted it, we even explained it to others, but in our own heart was a deep sense of perplexity and, if we were honest, a little anger.

Another root of perplexity may lie in disappointment as to what we have achieved in our ministry – in our work for God. It may be that as well as our job in the factory we have given time to teenagers. But the youth group that we used to lead is now scattered, and whereas at one time we believed these young men and women were going to grow into strong faith in Christ, it now appears they are disinterested. When we meet them in the street they seem embarrassed and mumble their reasons why they don't come to church any more. We look at a younger set of teens waiting to join our group and we wonder if we've got the stamina to do it all again when there seems such little fruit for our labours.

It may be you are a church leader. When you accepted the invitation to join your church you were sure that it was what God wanted. The people were welcoming, they promised to help with housing and babysitting, and constantly told you that God had answered their prayers in sending you. The honeymoon lasted six months: they never did get you the house they promised, they didn't manage babysitting beyond the first week, and it seems the only way God will answer their current prayers is for you to be called to another church. It has all gone so very wrong.

You honestly believed the change of job was God's will for your life. It was abroad, in fact in

Africa, and you went willingly but after six months you became ill and had to return. You are devastated, embarrassed and perplexed.

You prayed so hard for your husband to find the faith that has so changed your life. Finally he agreed to come to church with you. To say it was an off day would be an understatement. The preacher, who is normally compelling, seemed half-asleep, the drama was embarrassing and the welcome committee looked like piranhas in suits. When you got home he swore never to bother again.

There are no easy answers to such situations but part of the answer may lie in a sermon I heard when I was a teenager: the heart of it remains with me 30 years later. The preacher talked about 'The non-fairytale ending of the will of God.' He said that in life today happy endings are mandatory, but God sometimes looks at things from a different perspective. He takes a longer view, he is not in so much a hurry as we are and, furthermore, he has a way of achieving things through brokenness that are harder crafted when we feel all is well. For that very reason we cannot say to the person who had to return from Africa after just one month 'Ah, it obviously wasn't God's will for you to go there.' It may just have been God's perfect will.

Even more sobering is the fact that we cannot look at times of our life when things seem to be going well and presume we are therefore in the centre of God's will. If you are a business person be careful of saying 'I must be doing what I should, look how my business is prospering.' His ways are higher than ours and his thoughts higher than our thoughts.

And we may be perplexed because of personal circumstances. Our family life may be very difficult, our children are a disappointment to us or we are in financial difficulty. It may be that we are a single person and our career is not going well – in fact we have been demoted. Our friendships seem awkward and unfulfilling. Life is not good. It is easy at such times to lose heart and in so doing to lose our faith in God.

Those of us brought up in the Western world have been infected with a belief that makes all of this especially difficult. This belief is quite different to that taught to the majority of Christians through church history and yet in our culture it seems so fitting. It is simply that God exists to make us happy. When life goes well we feel close to him, when it goes badly we feel distant. And it is right here that one of the most fascinating of Jesus' parables may have something to say to us: 'Some [seed] fell on rocky places, where it did not have much soil. It sprang up quickly, because the soil was shallow. But when the sun came up, the plants were scorched, and they withered because they had no root' (Matthew 13:5). The sun speaks of persecution, of hard times, and the fascinating thing is the same sun that caused the good seed to grow caused the seed in shallow ground to die. Somebody says, 'Since I became a Christian, life has got worse, my family is going through a difficult time, my business is suffering, I can't go on in this faith.' And somebody else in even worse circumstances says, 'Thank God that I know him; if I didn't I could never get through it all.'

Not all our prayers will be answered with 'Yes'. Not all our children will turn out as we want, not all our churches will grow as we had hoped, and most of us will know times of crushing doubt. If you and I are to finish the course we are going to have to somehow learn how to hold on to God when our circumstances scream at us that there is no good reason to do so. This is not a new experience. Habakkuk wrote over three thousand years ago of this very period in our lives.

> Though the fig tree does not bud
> and there are no grapes on the vines,
> though the olive crop fails
> and the fields produce no food,
> though there are no sheep in the pen
> and no cattle in the stalls,
> yet I will rejoice in the Lord . . .
>
> (Habakkuk 3:17–18)

This is not an easy-believism joy. This is not frivolous. This is not easy. This is faith that is tried whilst standing by a grave, or in unemployment, or when our children are breaking our hearts; it is faith that rises out of the ashes of our deepest disappointments. Sometimes at our lowest moments this faith sneaks up on us because we have nowhere else to go, and as surely as night follows day everyone of us will come to a place at some time in our lives where we go on believing, not just because God seems good to us, but in spite of the most crushing perplexity. At that moment alongside the giant of doubt comes the child of faith that ultimately looks up and cries, 'I don't understand but I still trust you.' At our lowest moments it may even allow us to cry out with Job 'Though he slay me, yet I will hope in him' (Job 13:15).

At the moment we 'see but a poor reflection as in a mirror' (1 Corinthians 13:12) but one day we will have perfect vision and understanding. And remember when we stand before him there will be some surprises. The work we did that seemed so fruitless may look a little different from that perspective, the disappointments of today may take on a different colour in five years time, but perhaps even more so from the view of another world. And who knows what changes may be in store for the child who today breaks our heart; perhaps in parenting, as in life, we shouldn't read the score at half-time.

I am convinced that in spite of who I am inside, God is not finished with me yet. One woman put it like this:

> 'I know it all and I still love you.' That is the convincing, convicting, liberating truth that comes from an encounter with Christ. 'All is known. There is no need to pretend anymore.' I wrestled with that truth, but it is hard to lay aside a mask when it looks so like you and you have worn it so long that you can't remember what you looked like without it.[2]

Oh those masks that hide the real us from others, and even from ourselves. Like the circus clown we smile whilst our hearts are breaking:

> I have played the part so long,
> Worn the make-up and the smile.
> Took the bow and the applause,
> Said, 'Oh fine, oh, yes, of course ... I'm fine.'
>
> Donned the costume, trod the boards,
> Learnt the lines and sung the song,
> Made you laugh and made you cry.
> I have done it all so long ...
>
> I have done it all so long,
> That I don't expect you see,

That to get this leading role,
The real cost was ... me.[3]

You can take the mask off. God loves you. That is the simple, irrational truth. It is true if you feel him so close you could reach out and touch him. It is true if, at this moment, you are in deep despair and he seems so very distant. It is true if you have no love for him, or if you have lost the love that was once so dear to you. You may not believe in God – but God believes in you. He loves you.

There are many writings that have inspired me but the following two pieces are amongst my favourite prose in the whole world. The first comes from John White and is from the introduction to his book *The Fight*. It sums up so much of what we have considered together.

As you live the Christian life, you may have periods of darkness or of doubt. You may encounter painful struggle and discouragement. But there will also be moments of exultation and glory. And most important of all, you will become free.[4]

And the second is from the words of Paul, the man who had such a keen sense of his own frailty, but who eventually fought a good fight, and who, by God's grace, finished the course.

Therefore we do not lose heart. Though outwardly we are wasting away, yet inwardly we are being renewed day by day. For our light and momentary troubles are achieving for us an eternal glory that far outweighs them all. So we fix our eyes not on what is seen, but on what is unseen. For what is seen is temporary, but what is unseen is eternal.

(2 Corinthians 4:16–18).

In so far as is possible, be a bearer of hope, don't lose heart, and don't ever give up.

---

[1] Helen Mallicoat, 'I Am', in Tim Hansel, *Holy Sweat* (Dallas, Texas: Word, 1987), p.136.
[2] Sheila Walsh, *Honestly* (London: Hodder & Stoughton, 1996). Used with permission.
[3] Poem by Rob Parsons.
[4] John White, *The Fight* (Downers Grove, Illinois: InterVarsity Press, 1977).

SIGNPOST
INTERNATIONAL

Signpost International is a Christian Charity working with children and families at risk around the world. Signpost International tries to share the gospel in word and action through child sponsorship, house building, job creation schemes, building and equipping schools and working with street children, and through church-based missions, evangelism and short and long-term mission opportunities.

Signpost International: Changing Lives!

by Fiona Dixon

We attracted a large crowd of onlookers as we walked cautiously through the tightly packed streets of the shanty town – we were probably the first white people to ever venture into this poor community, and Filipinos are naturally curious. Some shouted 'Hey Joe, where are you going?' (a saying from the time when American GIs were stationed in the Philippines). Others shouted 'Hey you, give me money.' We kept walking, followed by a growing group of excited children, and even some adults, who obviously had nothing else to do that day.

In the shanty areas houses are packed together in a maze of pathways and narrow streets to make use of every available inch of space. Essentially the people are squatters, living on government land that no one else wants. Washing and shabby advertising banners for various brands of beer, gin and cigarettes hung from the windows, and it was often necessary to duck to avoid some obstacle hanging down into the street. Waste littered the walkways and we were very careful where we put our feet. The smell of sewage was strong and the occasional rat could be seen investigating the piles of rubbish. Cats, dogs and chickens wandered freely around the pathways, while enormous pigs sat and squealed in bamboo cages barely as large as they were.

We finally reached our destination – the house of a little girl called Christian Mae Flores – and went in. The house was tiny – just one very small room – and here the family of five lived, cooked, ate and slept, surrounded by their entire worldly belongings packed into a couple of tatty cardboard boxes. I had come with an English friend to visit Christian Mae and to check all was well with her and her family. Caroline and I, and the family's pastor, joined the Flores family in sitting crammed together on the floor. A baby slept soundly inside a triangle of material, suspended from a hook in the roof. Our Filipino interpreter stayed outside – he was worried that the house could not take the weight of the increased numbers of people.

The pastor, now acting as interpreter, explained that the family was ashamed that they could not offer us any food or drink by way of hospitality, but money was tight just now. Looking around us, that was obvious. The tiny house was not even strongly built – the bamboo flooring was rotten and unsafe, the wooden sides of the house had gaping holes in them, and the roof leaked.

Despite the appearance of her home and the surroundings she lived in, Christian Mae was actually one of the 'lucky' ones. She was being sponsored through school by a family in the UK, and this money enabled her parents to pay Christian Mae's monthly school fees, buy her school uniform, books and pens, and contribute a little rice each month towards the family's food. As we talked I discovered that Roland Flores, the father, earned just £1 per day in his job as a tricycle driver, taxiing people around in a rented push-bike and sidecar. This money just about paid for the rice needed each day by the family. Although a large sack of rice cost two weeks' wages, it would actually feed the family for a month, but the family could never save up the money needed to buy a sack of rice and lived hand to mouth, always hoping to earn enough to eat that day. Rent for the ramshackle house was £5 per month and 'extras', like education for the children, would have been forgone if it wasn't for the sponsors of Christian Mae. The Flores family was a perfect example of a family caught in the poverty trap, with no way of ever getting out.

It surprised me that the Flores family did not complain at all, instead talking with real gratitude of their thanks to God for the money they were receiving for Christian Mae. I, on the other hand, felt deeply ashamed at my comparative wealth and the security money brings. I was also frustrated at the Flores' situation and my inadequacy to help them.

I had given up my job in tax accountancy a few months earlier when I was aged 28 and moved from the beautiful south-west of England to Iloilo City in the central Philippines. I was spending a year working as a volunteer for Signpost International, a UK-based Christian charity, looking at their child sponsorship scheme in the Philippines and seeing where any changes needed to be made. I really wanted to know what God had planned for my life, and this seemed to be the direction he had sent me in. I had been feeling dissatisfied with my life and career in Exeter for a few years and I was hoping God had more in store for me!

Although I had travelled overseas before, the initial contrast between tranquil springtime in England and the noisy tropical Philippines was a shock. The humid night air hit me as I walked out of the air-conditioned airport at Iloilo, and within minutes the clothes that had been too light and chilly for an English April day were hot, wet, uncomfortable and sticking to my skin.

I was given a wonderful welcome by English and Filipino Signpost staff, who put a garland of flowers round my neck and waved a banner of welcome. They took my bags and 12 of us squeezed into an 8-seater van that took us to the house where I would be living for the next year. As we bumped over ill-made roads, weaving (dangerously, it seemed to me) through lanes of traffic, horns blaring, I tried to take in the sights and sounds of the Philippines. What looked like mostly unfinished concrete buildings stood side by side with flimsy shacks that appeared to be made out of waste materials. Children in dirty threadbare clothes played outside, despite the lateness of the hour, and adults sat drinking, gambling and gossiping. Emaciated dogs tried to steal food from the rickety stalls that lined the road, selling strange things like barbecued chicken claws, whole roast pigs and hard-boiled eggs containing chicken embryos.

The Filipina sitting next to me shyly introduced herself as Sister Nelly. She was also to be my language teacher.

'Look at the electricity wires. Do you have them like that in England?' she asked.

I looked where she pointed – masses of cables hung low over the street. Some had snapped and hung down into the road, the naked wires clearly visible. It looked incredibly dangerous to me.

'No', I said, 'it's not like that in England.'

When we got to the house I excused myself and went to bed as soon as was polite. I felt overwhelmed. Although I had a pillow and a sheet to cover me, I did not want them – the heat was unbearable and sleep impossible. My fan whirred round next to my bed but didn't seem to cool me down, only making the room worse, like a giant fan oven. Waves of panic started to flood over me, and I thought I would suffocate. Before I slept I began to pray. *Why am I here, God*? I whispered. *How can I cope with this for 12 months*? *Help me*. It just seemed like a very big mistake.

When I told Roy and Denise, Signpost's UK partners in the Philippines, about the state of the Flores' house, they decided a new house could be built for the family, a gift from Signpost's housing scheme. So, within two months of our initial visit, Caroline and I found ourselves back in the community helping with building work!

The new house was reached by walking along a (sometimes precarious!) raised bamboo walkway, as it was built beside the river where the water levels could rise with the tide. The house was simply but sturdily made from timber and plywood, with a corrugated sheet tin roof to keep out the rain. Like the walkway, the house was also built above the reach of the water, on concrete stilts. This six-foot elevation caused Caroline and I some problems as we nailed split bamboo to floor beams and painted the walls, often losing nails, paintbrushes and tools into the mud below – on a few occasions we had lucky escapes ourselves!

The regular daily appearances of the white female 'carpenters' caused much hilarity and meant large crowds often gathered to watch us at work (unfortunately these were the times that the nails bent as we hit them, or we hit our own thumbs!). However, our amateur attempts to help meant that we were quickly accepted into the community in a way that would not usually be possible. Men showed us the right way to use a saw, women chatted to us as they went about their daily washing, and normally shy children combed and plaited our strange Western hair and exclaimed at the size of our noses! More importantly, these new friendships gave us plenty of opportunities to explain why we had come to the Philippines, and so to share the gospel.

Often this was the way new outreaches started amongst a community: by building a house for a needy family; sponsoring a child through school; or providing financial assistance for much-needed medical treatment or an operation. These practical demonstrations of Christ's love in a situation would spill over into the close-knit Filipino communities and change lives. As a result, people came to know Christ and new churches were born. I once watched Roy tell a dispossessed widow that Signpost would build her and her family a new home.

Neneng showed real gratitude as he explained what the simple house would be like, adding, almost as an afterthought, that the house exterior would be painted green to help protect the plywood walls. At this, Neneng started to sob uncontrollably, and for a few minutes all she could do was point to heaven and say, 'Praise God!' This might seem like a strange thing to cry about when God had just provided her with a whole house, but this small extra touch from God in Neneng's life convinced her of the depth of God's concern, and for a few moments overwhelmed her with the reality of his love.

My memories of the day we dedicated the Flores' new house to God will always stay with me. In some small way I felt like I had shared in the family's poverty and seen God's miraculous provision of a house in a really personal way. The whole community was there, eating the snacks provided and talking about the new house standing in front of them. I had never seen so many smiling faces before!

We held a very simple service of dedication and worship, everyone laying hands on the house as we prayed for the family that was to live there, and thanked God for his love for them. On behalf of his family Roland Flores shyly testified to what God had done and cried tears of gratitude. People standing around

Roland cried with him – we were so overcome with the love, presence and power of God that day. Words were not enough to show how grateful we were.

Several times during my year in the Philippines it was necessary to visit the sponsor children living on the war-torn southern island of Mindanao. Here militant Muslims fought the Philippine army for independence, using guerrilla warfare and kidnappings to push their demands. Much caution was needed when travelling in that area.

Despite the dangers I was eager to go to Mindanao, specifically to visit the tribal people called the T'Boli who lived in the remote hills above beautiful Lake Sebu. I had heard a lot about these people, their animistic beliefs and rituals, and how they had first heard the gospel eight years before when Signpost's founder, Kerry Dixon, had been taken there to preach to them. The poverty he saw there, and the numbers of children dead and dying from curable diseases, had shocked Kerry. It was really from the needs seen during that visit that Signpost International began. Feeling incredibly inadequate in the face of such poverty, Kerry was asked to preach to the gathered tribe by the light of flaming torches. Through a chain of two interpreters, Kerry talked about God and his power in saving people from their lives of sin and suffering. When he had finished speaking the T'Boli people told Kerry that they were prepared to accept this God as their God if his power could be shown through the healing of a man from the village who had been blind since birth. All too aware of how he was completely dependant on God's mercy, Kerry prayed over the man three times, and the third time he prayed the whole tribe erupted. The blind man had been miraculously healed and a new church was born that night.

Despite the subsequent help Signpost has been able to give through projects such as child sponsorship and the housing scheme, the T'Boli tribe remain essentially a poor people. Some decades previously the T'Boli had owned the land that they lived on and farmed this land to provide a living. However, they had no ideas for business or the future and other more enterprising Filipinos came and bought the land from the T'Boli for low prices. By the time the money had been spent, the T'Boli people were being exploited as cheap labour by the new landowners, and they had to struggle daily to survive.

I arrived at the T'Boli village of El Lumet by Skylab (the name for an ordinary motorbike used as a public taxi service over rough terrain). In order to maximise profits Skylab drivers would often squeeze as many as five passengers (with luggage!) on to their bike for hair-raising rides into the mountains. Going fast over unmade roads certainly explained why this mode of transport was called Skylab, and I was always amazed there were as few accidents as there were. I certainly learned to cling on to the bike with every available part of me!

Electricity had not yet reached the village of El Lumet. All cooking was done over an open fire and flaming rags in jars of kerosene gave light when needed after sundown. The village toilet was a small pit in the ground, inadequate sacking surrounding it as a privacy screen – I decided to wait until dark before using it, as most Filipinos I had met were usually fascinated about whether I really was 'white all over'! The houses of the village were mostly in poor repair, made from the woven branches of palms and large leaves. The few chickens and animals wandering around and the general look of the people themselves showed how poor this village really was.

The local pastor – much to the amusement of the locals – placed me on a pony saddled with only an empty rice sack, and we set off to visit the families of the sponsor children of El Lumet. Despite their poverty the T'Boli people, like the majority of Filipinos, are sacrificially generous with what little they have. Everywhere we went the families offered us the best of what they had as hospitality – rice cakes, crackers and boiled corn on the cob. I was relieved at the food offered to us – I knew how poor these people were, and that necessity and hunger sometimes meant they ate things strange to Western tastes! I had come armed with a stock of T'Boli phrases and was pleased I could say *'Dou boloy Fiona, tay klegal lo ne delo uu'* ('My name is Fiona, I'm pleased to meet you') rather than *'Be gebenlay-ou bekong ne onge abay le noyu-udo'* ('Don't give me lizard and rat to eat because I don't like it!'). The laughter at my attempts to speak T'Boli soon got rid of any shyness the families felt at being visited by a white stranger, and it was good to hear how God was working in the lives of the families I visited that day.

That night, when sunset meant all work in the fields must stop, an all-night celebration service was held in the little church of El Lumet. The bamboo church had been built after Kerry's initial visit a few years ago and sat on top of a hill overlooking the houses of El Lumet. I sat in the church and watched hundreds of torches spread out into the distance, pinpricks of light, as the villagers of El Lumet made their way up the hill to worship God. It was amazing to me how many people packed into that small church and on to the wooden benches. One of the Filipino pastors explained to me that over 90 per cent of the villagers were Christians and that those who could had come here tonight for a special celebration of God's goodness. The T'Boli women looked fantastic in their traditional costumes of

embroidered shirts and lavishly beaded neck-
laces and headdresses. Sleepy children came
with their mothers, and a row of sleeping babies
soon lay in cloth triangles suspended from the
roof of the church.

The service began and people sang and
danced (with difficulty!) between the packed
benches. People stood up to give testimony to
God's goodness and blessing in their lives and
I found it incredible that, seeing their lives of
hardship and poverty, they could do this and
mean it! But it was obvious these people did
mean it and that in the midst of their poverty
they had discovered a quality of relationship
with God that few wealthy people ever will.

I never knew an all-night service could be so
enjoyable, or pass so quickly. One by one the
T'Boli brought their offerings to the front and,
as well as small amounts of money, it was
touching to see other gifts being brought forward: bags of rice, fish – even a couple of live
chickens were tethered to the front of the
church. I knew some families there might not
eat tomorrow because of what they had given
to God today.

Richard Wallis, visiting El Lumet from
Signpost's UK base, had been asked to speak to
the congregation that was now packed tightly
into the church building, spilling out into the
night. As he stood up to talk in the torchlight,
there came the loud noise of a sudden crack

from one of the church's high bamboo ledges, and a row of eight sleeping children tumbled out of the church on to the dark hillside. The small church had literally split open with the mass of people crammed inside. After initial consternation, the bewildered children were brought back into the building none the worse for their fall. The congregation had literally grown too big for the church building!

Back at home, in Iloilo City, I usually had a couple of language lessons in Hiligaynon – the local dialect – each week. I enjoyed the lessons, but was usually confused by some aspect of the grammar or pronunciation; as a result my favourite lessons were the ones when I managed to sidetrack Sister Nelly into talking about Filipino cultural differences instead!

One morning, unusually, Sister Nelly didn't come to the house for my usual language lesson. Most Filipinos tend to operate on 'Filipino time' – 'late', by Western timekeeping standards! – but Sister Nelly was usually very reliable. Later that day we had a telephone call – Sister Nelly's oldest son, Oskar, had been in a motorcycle accident and was seriously ill in hospital. We went to the hospital, where Oskar lay in intensive care, to comfort Sister Nelly and ask what we could do to help.

This was my first close encounter with Filipino hospitals – places where people were not treated unless they could pay the fees required, and armed security guards made sure patients did not leave with outstanding hospital debts. (Health insurance was available to those who could pay, but most Filipinos, living hand to mouth, could never afford this 'luxury'.) Seriously ill patients lay on stretchers in the hospital corridors, waiting to see if their relatives could guarantee payment of hospital costs before they were admitted to the basic wards, and all around me was misery and suffering of a kind that I had never seen before. Relatives slept in the corridors to be on hand to nurse their sick, and they brought in food from home to feed the patients when they were hungry.

When we eventually found her, Sister Nelly was distraught, but focusing on contacting friends, family and neighbours to beg and borrow money to pay the constant stream of hospital bills being presented to her. I was horrified at what was expected of the patients' relatives – while I was there, a prescription for medical essentials like intravenous drips, drugs and needles was given to Sister Nelly by a nurse, and she had to go around the city to various chemists until she had purchased everything. Relatives needed to be fundraisers, nurses, caterers and carers at a time of huge distress and trauma. It seemed incredible to me that Sister Nelly was coping as well as she was.

Oskar had lost a leg and a lot of blood in the accident, and had bad liver damage. He had regained consciousness, but the prognosis wasn't good for his recovery. A new prescription was brought in to Sister Nelly, this time for more blood to replace the blood lost in the accident, and we set off in our van to buy what was required.

It took us four hours, in Iloilo City's sweltering heat and noisy traffic congestion, to drive from hospital to hospital, asking for the quantity and type of blood Oskar needed. I wanted to know why we couldn't telephone ahead to see if the hospitals had this blood in stock before driving there fruitlessly, but was told this was not possible. Filipino bureaucracy and red tape baffled me sometimes.

We eventually found a hospital that had what Oskar needed. We bought the blood and drove slowly back through the city's traffic – exhausted, no one in the van spoke. I sat looking at the two precious packets of blood, bright red in the sunlight, rapidly defrosting in the tropical heat that still defeated the van's air-conditioning system. The whole situation was just incredible to me, like being caught up inside a nightmare. I did my best not to cry. Two weeks later, despite all the efforts made on his behalf, Oskar died.

Sister Nelly was beside herself – she had lost her son, and was also faced with massive hospital debts that she could not possibly meet. Now the hospital was refusing to release Oskar's body for burial until the bills had been paid. I was furious – with the system, the hospital and most of all with God.

'How can God say he cares,' I asked Sister Nelly, 'if he leaves you like this, with no son and no money?'

Sister Nelly was unwavering. 'God has not left us, and he will meet our needs.'

Unconvinced, I went home angry, challenging God to prove himself to me. Later that day I read an e-mail from my father. People in the UK had been touched by my e-mails about Oskar's accident and had given money to help. He would transfer it to my account immediately. I was delighted and ashamed – God was good and I was wrong! Nevertheless, it was a good lesson to learn. The hospital was paid, Oskar's body was released, and Sister Nelly buried her son.

I was envious of the attitude of my Christian Filipino friends towards God in their poverty. I was not convinced that, in their position, I would be the same. It felt like they had tapped into some spiritual secret for contentment that eluded me! One day I talked to my friend Ariel about this.

'Look at me,' he said. 'Before I knew God I was poor. My father was very sick and we could not afford his medicines. I could not go to school, as we could not pay the fees. My cousin and I scavenged in the rubbish heaps to find scrap to sell for food. But when I met God, everything was different!'

Confused, I questioned Ariel further. 'So what changed? Was your father healed? Did your financial circumstances improve?'

Ariel shook his head. 'No. I was still poor and my father was still sick. I still scavenged in the streets and could not go to school. But now I knew that God loved me and was with me in my sufferings. I could not ask for more! Nothing had changed, but everything was different.'

These incredible words went round and round in my head for weeks. 'Nothing had changed, but everything was different.' How could that be so? I had come to the Philippines to help in the poverty and need, but had just realised my own inadequacies all the more! I realised that the people I had come to help were helping me, showing me a new kind of relationship and dependency on God. I was deeply grateful to God for showing me these things.

At the present time your plenty will supply what they need, so that in turn their plenty will supply what you need. Then there will be equality (2 Corinthians 8:14).

FAITHWORKS

The Faithworks Movement is a robust response to the challenges facing churches and faith-based projects as they engage in their communities. It is built around 10 leading organisations that have committed to Faithworks and to each other to provide expertise and leadership in the many components of effective community action. Many leading denominations and church networks have joined the Faithworks Movement, determined to ensure that churches across Britain can benefit from the resources that Faithworks makes available.

Published by
KINGSWAY COMMUNICATIONS LTD
Lottbridge Drove, Eastbourne, BN23 6NT, England.
Email: books@kingsway.co.uk

The Thornbury Centre, Bradford

As told to and introduced by Steve Chalke

The church has an indispensable role to play in building communities and providing welfare up and down our land. That's the simple yet profound message of the Faithworks movement. Because churches are locally based and able to adapt imaginatively to the issues that surround them, their capacity to transform local neighbourhoods is unrivalled. No one is better placed to deliver the vital practical and spiritual hope which every individual and community needs in order to thrive.

Stories of Hope is the second book from Faithworks. It tells eight stories from churches of different denominations across the UK who are effectively tackling a wide range of social issues. From debt advice to counselling for domestic violence, from after-school projects to sports clubs, from education to youth work and from arts initiatives to vocational training

– each chapter tells an inspiring story of a
local church or individual that has responded
to a God-given sense of purpose and direction.

Told in the words of the people concerned, the
stories are open and revealing accounts of
the struggles and joys, challenges and opportunities, frustrations and breakthroughs of a faith
that has changed a community. There is much
we can learn from them. The imaginative solutions brought to the different needs they face,
the way in which common themes start to
emerge and the examples of working in partnership with local government and other
agencies, all help to point the way for those of
us with a desire to bring new hope to our local
communities.

The story of Paul Hackwood and the Thornbury Centre in Bradford is just one of
them.

Faithworks: Stories Of Hope is published by
Kingsway, 2001, and is priced £6.99.

* * *

*Paul Hackwood was appointed as chair of the
Thornbury Centre in June 1997. The centre, which
has been set up by the church of which Paul is vicar
and is run in association with a range of other*

organisations in the area, plays a unique role in restoring and rebuilding relationships in what has become a very divided urban community. It hosts a wide number of projects including an arts initiative, Artswork, work with the elderly, training pro-grammes and Homestart, part of a national initiative to support family life. Now aged 40, Paul is married to Josie. They have two children aged six and three.

Thornbury is a suburb one-and-a-half miles to the east of Bradford city centre. It is the second most disadvantaged ward in Yorkshire and suffers from high levels of poverty and crime. The community, which is very multicultural, has seen steadily increasing racial tension and violence in recent months.

Crime has become so endemic here that most people are largely unable to confront it. It has become almost impossible for those who would like to make a stand against it to do so in practice. The police are wary of getting involved in situations where they may be accused of being biased in favour of one racial community over another. They find themselves working against huge odds with few resources. It has become very difficult for them to police the area effectively. Our community has become a place where people have to live fairly heroic lives if they are to do the best for themselves and their families.

Thornbury has the second highest rate of drug arrests in Bradford (which is itself one of the worst areas for drug use in the country). The drug problem is, in turn, a big factor in the high level of HIV and Aids in the area. Another problem is the escalation of vandalism and property crime. Within the first month of our community centre being open we suffered £15,000 worth of theft and damage. There is also a lot of intimidation and violence. For instance, our church youth group had to be closed down after a member of our staff was stabbed there.

The decay in the community is so great that it has become accepted as the norm. For example, those who do not take drugs are often considered abnormal. I work with one young lad in his early 20s who decided 12 months ago to give up drugs and go to a rehabilitation clinic. Having returned clean, he is now quite often stopped on the street and beaten up if he refuses to buy drugs from the dealers. The whole context of the community works against him breaking free.

My office overlooks a primary school playground. A few weeks ago I looked out of my window to see two young lads selling drugs outside the school gates. People would walk up to them and hand over some money and be given a little package of white powder in return. It was particularly shocking to see this happen so flagrantly outside a school. So I went over and asked them to move. When they refused, I decided to stay with them and point out that they wouldn't be able to sell many drugs with a vicar standing next to them! They responded by calling their mates on their mobile phones, and the next thing I knew I was surrounded by 30 or 40 muscular lads jostling around and trying to intimidate me.

I was feeling quite fearful for my safety. However, I didn't feel I could back down and so I said, 'No matter what you do I am not going to move from here until you leave.' They became increasingly aggressive and got right to the point of physically assaulting me. However, just at that moment, a local Muslim leader drove past and stopped to see what was going on. When I explained what I was doing, he decided to stand with me. He told the youths (some of whom were also Muslims) that he too would not leave until they went. Eventually, they gave up and, after spitting on us both, moved on.

This story is typical of the kind of intimidation and lack of respect for the law that is common-place here. Working in Thornbury raises huge questions about how the Christian faith works in this kind of context. How does our understanding of God relate to an inner-city community that is fragmented, lawless and where nothing seems to go right? As I've thought this through, I have come to believe that because God is at work in the world, if the church is not engaged at the centre of the neighbourhood, then it is failing to participate in his mission. I have become convinced that unless we make the choice to step out of old models of being the church into new ones then our congregations will continue to dwindle and die.

I feel that in a very real sense God has been preparing me for my role here in Thornbury over many years. I grew up in the Midlands, near Birmingham, and started going to church at the age of 13. I trained as a social worker before being ordained. Over the years my experience of church has been very broad and I have worked and worshipped in all sorts of environments from Anglo-Catholic congregations through to charismatic evangelical ones. In my last job I was a social responsibility officer in St Albans, and when I was appointed to St Margaret's in Thornbury in June 1997, I knew I had the opportunity to try and implement the sort of project that I had been able to help others set up down there.

The site of the Thornbury Centre has been home to St Margaret's Church since the beginning of the 20th century. A traditional stone building was the base for the worshipping community until the late 1980s, when cracks started to appear in the chancel. Within a week a dangerous buildings notice was served on the PCC and as a result the whole building had to be demolished. This forced the congregation to move into an adjacent hall, and over the next few months to think carefully about the way ahead. Gradually, they came to the recognition that their church consisted of the people rather than the stone building. This was a very significant insight because it enabled them to see the value of their role as Christian people (not just a building) in the neighbourhood. Because of this, they decided that they didn't want to just build another church building, but rather to build a centre that would serve the wider community. It was out of this vision that the Thornbury Centre was born.

The church started to attract funding from a variety of different sources. The commitment of the congregation is shown by the fact that although they were a group of less than 50 people they managed to raise £250,000 between them. This was at the cost of much personal sacrifice (for example, I know pensioners on state pensions here who have tithed consistently for 10 years). They also managed to raise funding of a further £2.5 million through bodies such as the Millennium Commission, the European Union and the local Regeneration Development Agency.

It was at this stage that the existing vicar left and the Bishop of Bradford started looking for someone else who could develop the work. I was appointed on the basis of my previous experience, and I am now the vicar of the parish, as well as the chair of the centre. Since there was no building, my induction took place on the grassy site where the centre was to be built. Instead of a set of keys to the church I was given the plans for the building! One of my first jobs was to work with other members of the church to raise another £500,000 of funding, and then to turn the congregation's attention to getting the new building built and to setting in place the organisation and structure to run it.

Having started the building work in February 1998, it was finally completed in April of the following year, and officially opened by Princess Alexandra 12 months later. We asked the architect to design the centre in a way that made us open to the community as a church, but also giving us some private space that we could use together as a congregation. As a result, we have a very distinctive building. The architect has created an extremely light and airy building with a central atrium, which links all the rooms in the building. When you want to pass from one room to another you always have to walk through the central communal area. What that does is create connections and means that the ethos of our building is the same as that of our overall work – we are here to create connections between people.

As you enter the building you step into a cafeteria area. We wanted to have a space that welcomed people, and food is very welcoming. On the left is the worship area, which is entered through a stained glass door so as to give the impression of something special lying behind it. At the back of the building is a community hall and bar, used for local celebrations. As well as that we have seven meeting rooms of varying sizes. Some of these are used by the projects that work from the building, and others are let out to other local organisations and businesses in order to create some revenue with which to run the centre.

The Thornbury Centre's overarching goal is to tackle the underlying problems that threaten the community. I believe that the core issues are far deeper than the lawless escalation of drugs, vandalism and violence. These problems are symptomatic of a greater underlying sense of hopelessness, caused by the lack of options for local residents, particularly for young people. When there are few jobs or prospects and unemployment runs at 25 per cent, how can you imagine a future of brighter possibilities? It's an environment that is corrosive and dehumanising. Without hope people cannot grasp the importance of having a system of values that will benefit anyone, or anything, beyond themselves. As a result, they tend to do things that centre on their own survival rather than working to develop community and relationships with their neighbours. And worst of all, it's a vicious circle because the resulting social fragmentation only reinforces the overwhelming sense of hopelessness.

A big part of what we are trying to do is to give people the opportunity to be hopeful about the future. I believe that it is a very important part of our Christian message to say that human beings are creatures of hope. As Christians, we believe that God is in the process of enhancing our humanity and making us the best we can possibly be. We believe that every human being is full of potential. We believe that God is slowly establishing a future that is positive. The Bible calls us to a vision of community where all live under God's authority and recognise the humanity and worth of others, enabling it to flourish; a community where all people live together in an atmosphere of peace, justice and truth. Without this vision of tomorrow there is no point in having any values because they have no ultimate goal to take us to.

We believe that the best way of empowering the local residents of Thornbury is to give them the opportunity to address their needs in their own way. As a matter of principle, we will not run a project unless it has been asked for by the community. A lot of our work continues to be based on the original audit that we did about four years ago in order to find out what people wanted in the building. However, we also regularly carry out door-to-door surveys because we want to keep listening to local people and to let them know that they have a voice.

We try wherever possible to ensure that any service that is provided in the centre is run by and shaped by local people. We work hard to give people a say in the management of the projects, and to ensure that they feel a real sense of ownership of them. We have set ourselves against creating any sort of relationship of dependency. It's not that we don't steer things and guide them, it's just that we don't steer and guide them in directions people don't want to go!

It has been difficult to find clear models for the kind of work that we as a church are engaged in. Models that focus solely on the congregation won't work for us, because they end up separating us from the community. But equally, models that are too heavily community orientated would end up destroying the congregation because the needs in the area are endless.

So our response has been to pray and look for the activity that God is already engaged in within Thornbury and try to join in. For instance, one area where we feel God is at work is in restoring relationships and unity within the community. So one of the things we are focusing on is building our relationship with other faith communities. We do not in any sense abandon our Christian perspective. However, we do recognise that because relationships across the ethnic communities are so bad they have a dehumanising influence on the whole of the neighbourhood. People are so alienated that, for example, the Muslims won't have any contact with the Hindus and Sikhs, whilst many young white British people won't even walk down streets where the Muslims live, and vice versa. We have tried to address these issues by working hard with the other religious communities. We have seen great progress and I believe that God's Spirit is at work creating a new sense of community in Thornbury. We have been fortunate to have a really good south Indian pastor, Solomon Joseph, working with another church in the area, who has been a guiding force behind much of this progress.

It has been very important to create the right governing structures at the centre. But because the church and the wider community use the same resource, perhaps there will always be a bit of a tension here. On one hand, we don't want to see the church dictate to the community, so we have tried to frame our constitution as carefully as possible. We have set up a charity that is made up of seven representatives from the church council, two from the local authority, three from the local community, four who represent the users of the centre, and one from the local school. What that means is that the church has a major say in what goes on (some of the user group representatives are also associated with the church), though legally we only have a third of the votes. Therefore we have to listen actively to what other people have to say, which I think is a good discipline because churches have often been guilty of setting their own agenda without really engaging with their communities. But we also have some level of protection because the constitution prohibits certain activities that would be inappropriate or against our values. For example, the worship of other communities is not allowed in the building and the incumbent has a say in whether or not any particular activity is conducive to the central ethos of building up the community. Since the constitution cannot be changed without two thirds of the votes there is a level of protection there, though we always try to work as openly with the community as possible.

We run a wide range of projects out of the centre. Some have been initiated by the church, while others are run by or in association with other organisations. They are all non-profit making, as required by the constitution, and whatever surplus they make gets ploughed back into the overall work of the centre. We are constantly on the hunt for new ideas. One person on our board also sits on the Local Regeneration Board Partnership, and if they identify any good project ideas that need a base to develop from, then we look to see whether or not they correspond with the kind of needs that local people have identified and whether they fit with our ethos. If there is a significant match then we will positively consider working with them.

One of the projects that we run out of the centre is called Artswork. It grew from the idea I had when I first arrived that there was a lot we could do to help local people foster their creativity. As we looked at the possibilities we came across a woman by the name of Bev Morton who had a very similar vision. As a result, we set the project up together. The aim is to help put local people who have creative ideas for regenerating the community into contact with professional artists in order to help them achieve their goal. Artswork has proved very successful, and over the last two years we have involved about seven thousand people in the initiative. In fact, it has grown so much that we have recently registered it as an independent charity. We have implemented a variety of ideas, from commissioning public art and sculptures for some of the local housing estates, right through to producing a local authority calendar each year, incorporating paintings and collages from both children and adults, and which is distributed to every house in the neighbourhood. Some of the paintings from the calendar have even been blown up and posted on roadside advertising hoardings right across the city. It is great when a local person who has never been given much opportunity to express their creativity sees their artwork as they ride somewhere on a bus or in a car. As you can imagine it gives them a tremendous buzz of pride and affirmation. Another thing Artswork does every year is to create puppets and costumes for the Bradford carnival – last year we had nine floats full of dressed-up people from the local estates in the procession!

We have developed our work with older people in partnership with the local council. Our community faces a considerable problem in relation to elderly people suffering from a sense of isolation, intimidation and fear. Because of the level of crime in the area, it is almost impossible to get them to come out after dark and in winter they can feel forced into staying in their homes for days on end. Our senior citizens' work is centred around Wednesdays. We start with a service at 10.00 a.m., which about 30 people come to, and afterwards have a luncheon club, which about 65 people now attend. The project has really taken off under its own steam and we don't have to do anything except provide the food. Many people then stay on for most of the afternoon. We have a local police officer who regularly pops in to chat about crime prevention issues. We also invite other speakers along – for instance, recently someone from the council came in to talk about benefits advice. We are presently looking at the possibility of setting up other leisure activities around the afternoon group. Once a month we also host a tea club, which runs a programme including invited speakers and feature films. The organising group also plans other community activities for their age group, such as day trips etc. We are now actively looking at how we expand this work.

The library is run by the local authority and hosted by us at the centre. We originally set it up as a neighbourhood information centre to facilitate communication between organisations like the council or the local health service and the residents. Our job was to act as the disseminator of lots of informative brochures and leaflets. But now, as a joint initiative, it has grown into a fully-fledged library staffed by a local authority librarian, assisted by a community resident. The idea behind this aspect of the scheme is both to build a bit more community into the library as well as provide a local person with some excellent training for the job market.

We place a big emphasis on training in the centre. For instance, Bradford College uses our facilities to teach a course in mature studies. This enables people with no educational qualifications to gain a foundation certificate within 18 months, which will then qualify them for university entrance. They also run a very popular English as a second language course. On top of that, we have an IT training suite that is run in partnership with the council. It comprises 24 computers, used to help local people upgrade their computer skills and gain qualifications. We run weekly courses in desktop publishing, word processing, spreadsheets and databases. We also run regular courses in various other skills, including such things as dressmaking and line dancing.

We run Homestart as part of a national initiative that uses volunteers to work alongside families who need support, for example, a parent who is struggling to cope with a child who is ill or who has behavioural problems, or a mum or dad that just need a bit of a break. Our volunteers are all fully trained in childcare and support, including child protection, and will commit to spending a morning or afternoon a week in each home working with the parent and acting as a carer. To supplement Homestart, we also run a nursery and childcare project called 'Child Works', and have a youth project that is supervised by the local authority.

Our café is open every day and has three aims. First of all it tries to create a heart for the centre. We try to provide a safe space where older and younger people can come and eat together in a public, but non-threatening, environment. For instance, one woman who comes was severely agoraphobic until the café opened, but now she feels comfortable enough to come in every day. Secondly, the café also enables us to train people in catering skills. We have had many local people who have qualified in food hygiene to NVQ level 2 and then gone on to find a permanent job. Thirdly, although the café itself runs at a loss, the catering service generates income – we do outside bookings for local businesses and community organisations, as well as internal work for training and conference events held in our building.

We also have a bar adjacent to the main hall. It is run by the church congregation and is used largely for community events. Once again, any profit it makes gets ploughed back into other church activities. The congregation also organises bingo in the hall as a community outreach and runs the Emmaus evangelism course for people who want to know more about the Christian faith, which we find always has a number of delegates who have arrived there via our other activities.

We have 15 full-time staff and a much larger number of volunteers. Twenty-five or so members of the congregation volunteer to work specifically for the centre. We treat all volunteers just as if they are employees. So although they don't get contracts of employment, they do receive job descriptions, supervision and appraisals, and are part of staff meetings.

We have worked hard to develop good relationships with other agencies that are engaged in delivering welfare in the community. Many of them have used our facilities and seem to like the physical attractiveness of the building and the fact that we create a space where they can come and work without any interference.

Our relationship with council officers is very good, and they have been supportive of us from the beginning. We have also developed good links with the Regional Development Agency. However, we have sometimes had a mixed response from some local community leaders, who have been very suspicious of us. When we have been attacked, the key has been not to fight back, but neither to compromise our objectives. We feel that the key is to do all we can to try and build good relationships with them by not looking for trouble, but at the same time to not allow ourselves to be intimidated.

We never use government money for evangelism, not only because the conditions of such funds specifically exclude this, but also because we would be uncomfortable with it anyway. We now have a turnover of half a million pounds per annum, but have worked hard at not becoming so dependent upon grants that our prophetic edge is undermined. We have, therefore, tried to create a one-third/two-thirds split. Although one third of our total income comes through grants such as the lottery, the other two thirds is self-sustained and made up from letting our facilities for conferences, as well as proceeds from the bar, the café and so on.

We believe it is morally wrong to make the use of any service dependent upon a faith allegiance. However, if we are asked, or if it is otherwise appropriate, we will always openly and honestly talk about what we believe. We never put a wrapper on our faith, which includes our dealings with the other faith communities, but neither do we push it insensitively.

If someone were to say that our work in the community is a distraction from our duty to evangelise, then I would say that they don't understand what evangelism is. Evangelism is about telling people the good news of Jesus Christ in a way that affects them both personally and socially. But it's a message that needs to be communicated through the things that we do, as well as verbally. In our society as a whole, and certainly in Thornbury, there are too many spoken words. It is only when people see that those words are backed up with integrity that they are really heard. I believe that it is no coincidence that our congregation numbers have almost doubled since we opened the centre.

What we are really trying to do is to create an alternative. I don't think we can ever change the whole world, or even, for that matter, the whole of Thornbury. But we can create an alternative that says there is a different way to live and relate to others; you don't have to live solely for your own survival; it's possible to live in a way where you trust others and are prepared to listen and work together with them. Of course, all this is a journey. If we could have seen 10 years ago what we are doing now, we would have been too afraid to begin. All we did back then was to take the one small step we could, and then another, and another, until we have reached the point where we are today. And that first step was simply trying to catch a vision for what was possible.

None of what we have done has been easy. In fact, it has been absolute agony. I have been repeatedly tested beyond my own strength and training, and sometimes it has challenged the very depth of my faith. One problem is the level of conflict that you get whenever you try to start something new. People can get very suspicious. They go to all sorts of lengths to check that you know what you're doing, and that you're able to deliver what you said you would deliver. They won't trust you. Then sometimes it all gets very personal. I have experienced some personal attacks that have left me absolutely devastated. Once I went through weeks when I hardly slept because I was so anxious about it all. In fact, I have lived through four years of self-doubt in a way that I would never have imagined was possible before.

To be truthful, I feel that I have been both challenged at a personal level as well as enriched by the Thornbury experience. And yet I know God has kept me going when I've most needed it. I can honestly say that without the empowering activity of God's Spirit, Thornbury would never have happened. There have been times when I've reached the point where I couldn't go on any further, and then I've felt a little nudge to keep me going as new possibilities have opened up.

As for my joys, it is a wonderful privilege to participate in what God is doing. And to that end, one of my greatest moments was last year when a local group of Muslim leaders said 'The Church of England is good news for this community.' Even if I don't carry anything else away from this place other than that, then it has been worthwhile.